KW-495-001

TABLE OF CONTENTS   Page

SUMMARY OF THE PROCEEDINGS

Suzanne THIBAL
General Rapporteur
Secretary General of EUROTER

This Colloquy was held in Larnaca at the instigation of the Council of Europe under its programme of co-operation with the countries of central and eastern Europe and with the support of the Cypriot authorities, particularly the Ministry of Agriculture, Natural Resources and Environment and the Tourism Organisation.

The Colloquy provided an opportunity for dialogue on the subject of "sustainable tourist development" between representatives of Albania, Belarus, the Czech Republic, Croatia, Estonia, Hungary, Latvia, Lithuania, the "former Yugoslav Republic of Macedonia", Moldova, Poland, Romania, Slovakia, Ukraine, and Rapporteurs from the host country, Cyprus, and from various NGOs and other institutions.

1.   OFFICIAL WELCOME

On behalf of the Cypriot government, Dr Avraam LOUCA, welcomed the participants to the Larnaca Colloquy, and stressed the importance and relevance of the theme of the colloquy, considering that all of the countries present were now confronted with the need for sustainable management of tourist development.

Dr LOUCA hoped that Cyprus's experience of tourism might contribute towards the work of the Colloquy whilst stressing that his country, in turn, would gain considerable benefit from the meeting.

2.   THE PURPOSE OF THE COLLOQUY

It fell to the Council of Europe representative to describe the background to the Larnaca Colloquy and its aims.

At the opening of the proceedings, Mrs Hélène BOUGUESSA, speaking on behalf of the Directorate of Environment and Local Authorities, began by sketching out the main principles and objectives behind the work of the Council of Europe since its foundation in 1949, and went on to outline the various activities undertaken since 1989 to support the new democracies of central and eastern Europe, particularly those carried out under the co-operation and assistance programmes. It was in the context of these programmes that the Larnaca Colloquy was being held, its aim being to encourage various European countries to exchange experiences and pool their ideas with regard to tourist development whether in western Europe, central Europe or around the Mediterranean.

And, with this goal in mind, Mrs Bouguessa asked the participants to:

- take account during their discussions of the degrading and destabilising effects of tourism which result from intense pressure on the environment and local populations alike;

- conduct in-depth cost-benefit analyses to calculate the real impact of tourism on local populations;

- identify new economic indicators which take account of external social and environmental factors ignored in economic statistics.

During the Colloquy, Mr Carlos PINTO, MP and member of the Committee on the Environment, Regional Planning and Local Authorities, drew on his dual experience as a parliamentarian at the Council of Europe and a local councillor in Portugal to illustrate his comments on tourist development.

He stressed that a country could only have a specific strategy for tourist development provided that the question of the economic, social and cultural benefits which the inhabitants and the local authorities could expect from tourism was raised as a prerequisite to any development.

While acknowledging that tourism could act as a driving force, Mr Pinto pointed out that the tourist trade was very closely linked with other economic sectors and this entailed adopting an overall inter-sectoral approach, setting up partnerships between public and private operators, establishing local co-operation and, hence, involving local authorities in tourist development.

With this purpose in mind, he said he was in favour of extending the scope of aid granted by the Council of Europe (and the European Union) to the newly emerging democracies to include sustainable local tourist development in Europe.

3.   THEMES OF THE COLLOQUY

3.1   Guidelines for the proceedings of the colloquy:

- The process of discussing "sustainable tourist development" implies dealing simultaneously with three aspects: the concept of development, tourist economics and the definition of sustainability.

- "Sustainable tourist development" is a function both of space and of time; therefore it is ultimately related to geo-physical, historical and cultural features.

- Another consequence of this is that "sustainable tourist development" forms part of the current world-wide debate on the ethical problems raised by the management of the global environment in response to the demands of human development.

—   Finally, since the Colloquy on "sustainable tourist development" was expected to produce practical results, case studies would be used to highlight the (positive and negative) impact of the interaction between the environment and the development of the tourist trade so as to identify, wherever possible, principles and rules which should govern our actions.

3.2   General concepts upon which the work of the Colloquy was based

—   The basic concept of "sustainable development".

The quest for harmonious, balanced development integrated into its surroundings or the host community is not, strictly speaking, a new development; sufficient proof for this can be found in the macro and micro-economic approaches which have characterised recent decades and which can be identified, in the tourist industry in particular, in the form either of major mass tourist sites or of dispersed local tourism.

Over the years numerous reports and colloquies have analyzed then praised or denounced the advantages and drawbacks, or even the negative effects, of each of these two patterns of development, according to the priorities and objectives attached to public, private, urban and spatial tourist facilities.

What is new in fact is that the whole world is becoming aware of:

-    the extent and the growing pace of the negative impact of development which is out of proportion or uncontrollable in relation to the receptive capacity of a site or a community;

-    the vulnerability of natural and cultural resources and the risk of destroying them;

-    the new demands expressed by people who now place a greater premium on quality than on quantity as much for themselves as for future generations.

And this applies as much to the tourist trade as it does to all the other sectors of human activity.

Admittedly, awareness of these matters varies from country to country according to their political, economic, social and cultural situations, their level of tourist development, their history and also the motivations of public or private tourist concerns.

This means that the same tourist development project can be considered in one region as a goal to be achieved and in another as a harmful process which has to be controlled.

The fact remains that two main reference works are now universally recognised as authorities on the subject of "sustainable development":

-   the Brundtland Report entitled "Our Common Future" published in 1987 by the United Nations Committee for Environment and Development, which was first put the idea of "sustainable development" on the map;

-   the "Agenda 21" action programme approved by 182 governments at the United Nations Conference on Environment and Development (UNCED) which was held as part of the "Earth Summit" in Rio on 14 June 1992.

One challenge and a number of principles are identified in these texts.

—   The challenge:

"the survival of Humanity and its well-being depend on the extent to which we can elevate sustainable development to the rank of a global ethos"[1].

—   Some of the principles:

-   sustainable development makes it possible to meet present needs without undermining the potential for future generations to meet theirs;

-   sustainable development is a process of change dealing in a harmonised way with the exploitation of resources, investment policies, the application of new technology and the development of institutions and business concerns with a view to enhancing the social and economic potential required to meet the needs and expectations of Humanity in the present and the future;

-   there is no ideal model for sustainable development, because political and economic circumstances and the environmental situation vary from one place to another, - what never varies is the quest for a state of harmony between human beings and the Earth's natural heritage.

—   "Sustainable tourist development"

"Agenda 21" therefore amounts to a master plan which, on the one hand, pinpoints problems of environment and development which may lead to economic and ecological (and hence human) disaster and, on the other hand, proposes a strategy for change using the development tools suited to preserving the Earth's resources into the twenty-first century.

Its application in the travel and tourist industry is the subject of a publication by the World Tourism Organisation (WTO - see p.12), which is currently being

---

[1]   See "L'Ethique de l'Environnement et du Développement", by José A. Prades, published in the "Que sais-je?" collection by Presses Universitaires de France, 1995.

distributed in a provisional version prior to final editing.

This programme proposes objectives and priority measures to be taken up on the one hand by Ministries, public bodies and other public organisations, and on the other hand by businesses. It includes:

-   nine priority objectives for the public sector, and;
-   ten for the private sector.

A special mention should be made of the recommendation to set up partnerships which is found in both sets of proposals.

—   Informative practical experience

The Colloquy having been placed in its conceptual context and having pointed out the issues and problems underlying "sustainable tourist development", the participants embarked on the practical, empirical and critical stage of the proceedings.

To this end, sector-by-sector reports had been prepared to be discussed in the light of:

-   the major theoretical principles comprising the new and widely-accepted global approach to the interaction between development and the environment known as "sustainable development";

-   the application of these principles to tourism, the working methods adopted, and the practical measures taken;

so that these practical experiences could be used as an example and conclusions could be drawn from them for the benefit of "sustainable tourist development in Europe".

4.   **TWO FORMER INTERNATIONAL APPROACHES TOWARDS THE ISSUE OF SUSTAINABLE TOURIST DEVELOPMENT**

—   The Mediterranean Tourism Charter, adopted by the Ministers of Tourism of the Mediterranean countries at the Casablanca Conference in September 1995 (presented by Mr Robert LANQUAR - Mediterranean "Blue Plan").

This activity was one result of the various joint meetings of Mediterranean countries held since the 1975 Barcelona Conference with a view to protecting their common heritage, based in particular on the Mediterranean "Blue Plan".

The aim of the Mediterranean Tourist Charter was to protect, enhance and promote the Mediterranean identity in the context of broad co-operation aimed at promoting the sustainable tourist development of the whole region and the well-being of the people concerned.

To this end the Mediterranean states had agreed to set up a "Mediterranean Tourism Network" as a tool for co-operation between States, local and regional authorities, tourist operators and consumers' associations; a plan for the structural organisation of this co-operation was currently being examined, based along three main lines: information, promotion and training.

—   The World Tourism Organisation

On behalf of the WTO, Mr Peter SHACKLEFORD drew attention to the specific nature of this international organisation and:

-        presented and commented on the world tourist statistics for 1994, comparing them with the growing share of the market won by central and eastern European countries (22% of total visitors and 6% of total receipts), which could pose dangers for the environment in the regions in question if tourist demands were not curbed;

-        pointed out that the WTO had an Environment Committee comprising 35 countries which, since 1990, had been developing a specific "Environment" programme aimed at promoting regional development through local planning, integrated resource planning, particularly in natural parks, and education and training. The programme would be implemented using various means including wide dissemination of the principles of environmental protection and 11 indicators by which the impact of tourism could be measured;

-        stressed that it was the WTO's role to implement the United Nations Programme for Technical Co-operation, in the form of special assignments: mass plans and master plans, cultural routes, marketing and management, training, eco-tourism, etc. He referred in particular to Agenda 21 (see p. 5) and its application to the economic aspects of tourism[2].

5.   SECTORAL REPORTS

5.1   Full reports and technical reports on tourist development in Cyprus, host country of the Colloquy and "typical example" for the discussion

5.1.1   Mr Patroclos A. APOSTOLIDES (Cyprus Tourism Organisation) described the current situation in Cyprus and the positive and negative effects of the growth of tourism in his country, before giving details of Cyprus's new national policy on tourist development which was currently being implemented.

---

[2]   see "Agenda 21 for the Travel and Tourism Industry - Towards Environmentally Sustainable Development", World Tourism Organisation (WTO)/ World Travel and Tourism Council (WTTC)/ Earth Council, Madrid, 1995).

CYPRUS:

- 3rd largest island in the Mediterranean - 9,250 km² - 790 km of coastline,
- two mountain ranges cross the island (highest summit: 1,951 m),
- the free part of the island covers some 600,00 hectares (one third of the island has been under military occupation since 1974),
- 68% of the population live in the capital and the coastal towns - 32% in the rural areas in the interior,
- economic contribution of tourism: 42% of exports - 21% of gross national product,
- 25% of jobs are related directly or indirectly to tourism,
- 2,070,000 visitors in 1994 (compared with 430,000 in 1980), 86% of whom were from Europe,
- 76,100 beds for tourists of which 71,000 are in coastal areas,
- Cyprus Tourism Organisation - a semi-public organisation, sponsored by the Ministry of Trade, Industry and Tourism.

Problems encountered:

- 1st stage: 1974-1981: period of reconstruction of the Cypriot economy following the events of 1974, particularly regarding the economic side of tourism;

- 2nd stage: 1982-1990: substantial growth in tourism (in the region of 20-22% per year) which gradually had a number of adverse effects (large-scale buildings along the coastline, a lack of means of public access to the coast, overcrowding in the high season, increases in the price of land and a reduction in the amount of suitable land for farming, coastal erosion, over-exploitation of water resources, various types of pollution, disfigurement of the landscape, problems with protecting archaeological sites on private property, changes in local habits and customs, the destruction of the village heritage and a decline in the rural population).

However, at the same time, the tourist boom also had a number of positive effects: income from tourism enabled local authorities to invest in useful facilities for the resident population, traditional arts and crafts were thriving, standards of living improved, tourist activities multiplied, jobs became more diversified, and the social and cultural links between the inhabitants and visitors increased.

- 3rd stage: in June 1989, faced with the scale of the recorded adverse effects of the tourist boom, and in response to the growing environmental awareness of the people, the Cypriot authorities ordered a moratorium on coastal tourist development, to give them time to devise a National Policy on Tourist Development.

Since 1990 a number of activities had been launched:

- development planning at national, regional and local level;
- classification of three vulnerable areas as "national parks" (other areas are under consideration);
- increased restrictions on tourist development within 3 km of the coastline;
- promotion of alternative forms of tourism and development of tourism in the interior;
- adoption and application of the principles of sustainable development in the use of Cyprus's natural and cultural resources for tourism.

In conclusion to his comments, Mr Apostolides stressed that the protection of natural and cultural resources required a radical change in people's ways of thinking and their behaviour and he felt that there was a duty to meet this challenge.

5.1.2   Mr N.S. GEORGIADES (Ministry of Agriculture, Natural Resources and Environment) gave some further information on the details of the Cypriot government's policy of environmental management.

- Their main frames of reference were:
  . sustainable development,
  . taking environmental factors into account in policies of social and economic development,
  . future integration into the European Union.

- Their main objectives were to:
  . preserve natural resources,
  . protect biodiversity and eco-systems,
  . eliminate damage caused to the environment,
  . consolidate existing institutional structures,
  . raise environmental awareness,
  . set up partnerships,
  . update and codify environmental legislation,
  . control pollution and waste management.

Mr Georgiades went on to describe the institutional framework which had been set up for regional development and environmental management (the constituent bodies, their role, their working methods and studies completed and under way).

In conclusion, he took stock of the present situation:

- positive aspects included: a major government programme on the environment, broad political backing for environmental protection measures, the support of the media and the awareness of the local population;

- negative aspects which needed to be remedied included: the preponderance of short-term goals and a lack of long-term prospects, too many activities with no order of priority, the need for training for civil servants, excessive individual involvement and conflicting private interests.

5.1.3   Mr Ermis KLOKKARIS (Department of Town Planning and Housing) presented the measures planned under the Town Planning and Development Act which provided for tourist plans (Country Site Policy, Local Plans, Area Schemes) and took stock of five years of implementation.

He felt that the triple objective of sustainable tourist development (controlling numbers, organising tourist areas and providing amenities, diversifying the product) were gradually being achieved, but further steps had to be taken with regard to regional planning, devising new products, drawing up local development plans, introducing new fiscal measures and rehabilitating developed zones by means of detailed planning.

5.1.4   Ms Xenia LOIZIDOU (Public Works Department) concluded by giving a highly informative talk on the various measures taken to protect the coasts of Cyprus against erosion (of natural or human origin) which she illustrated using slides.

5.2.   *Supervision and restrictions as pre-requisites for sustainable tourist development: 2 reports by Mr Tony ELLUL (Planning Directorate - Malta) provided food for thought on this subject.*

5.2.1   Tourist planning contributed to the protection of the environment by controlling tourist development.

Mr Ellul began by stressing that supervision should not be seen as a means of impeding tourist development altogether, but instead as a series of monitoring tools designed to help to make tourist development sustainable.

Accordingly, these supervisory measures should help to:

- protect the natural, cultural and social heritage;
- maintain the quality of life of the local population;
- offer tourists a high quality product;
- while still enabling tourist operators to secure a decent return on their investments.

Supervisory measures could be divided into six categories:

- planning policies (at national, regional and local level);
- regulatory procedures (particularly impact studies);
- economic measures in the form of financial incentives to encourage schemes which are in keeping with sustainable development or taxes penalising activities which are harmful to the environment;
- environmental indicators, resulting from the analysis of information gathered by means of inspections, checks, data bases, exchanges of experience, etc.;
- operational networks (tourist offices, professionals, etc.);
- voluntary schemes or the results of partnerships between the public and private sector (codes of conduct, promotional events, training sessions, exchanges of experience, etc.).

5.2.2   Legal measures should be introduced to help to manage problems of pollution caused by tourism.

Mr Ellul defined pollution as any activity which threatened the balance of the eco-system which was a changing relationship comprising elements which varied along with the fluctuations of energy and matter.

Pollution came in different forms and could be related to water, air, noise, waste, appearance and other factors, not forgetting the social pollution created by the excessive demands of tourism on the local population.

Sustainable development should make it possible to monitor and control pollution caused by tourist activities, particularly by means of legal measures. However, though legislation was important, it was not enough in itself to solve the problem. It should be accompanied and supplemented by voluntary schemes based on the principle of collective and individual responsibility; and, moreover, it should be borne in mind that a well looked-after environment augured well for the future of tourist development.

5.3   *Three practical experiences bearing lessons (presented, commented on and illustrated with slides)*

5.3.1   The example of the Aggtelek National Park in Hungary, presented by Mr Janos LERNER

Details:

- the smallest national park in Hungary (20,000 hectares) founded in 1985 on the site of a protected natural area, listed as a biosphere reserve in 1979 (karstic landscape, numerous caves, a large variety of flora and fauna);

14

- two villages are located within the boundaries of the park (1,000 hectares) and 12 others along the edges, based for the most part on agricultural activities;

- 200,000 visitors per year, concentrated in the areas around the cave entrances.

Problems encountered:

- conservation of the site entailed restrictive measures such as rules on grazing, forestry, agriculture and the spreading of chemical products in the fields, as well as prohibiting access to the central part of the biosphere reserve;

- the concentration of visitors in space and time as well as their behaviour had led to a deterioration of the site: litter, trampling, and breakage and erosion of stalactites and stalagmites, as well as the growth of parasitic plants as a result of the artificial light used in the caves;

- both the tourists and the local population found it hard to accept the restrictions on access and use of the site.

A balance had to be found between the protection of the site's natural resources, the vital interests of the local population, and the expectations of the tourists. This balance could only be achieved via a compromise, reconciling the diverse interests of the parties present on the site; and, to this end, the management of the national park could and should take on the role of mediator, interpreter and advisor, and provide information and training in order to achieve and preserve the necessary balance.

5.3.2   Protection of Estonian landscapes, by Mr Toomas KOKOVKIN (Hiiumaa Biosphere Reserve, Estonia)

Estonia, in its position in the centre of the European plain, contained a wide variety of natural landscapes, which had been shaped by cultural, political and social factors (ancient traditions of nature conservation, large-scale agriculture and the extension of woodlands, military restrictions on access to the coastline, which had upset the social traditions of the adjacent villages but also, paradoxically, contributed towards the protection of the natural environment).

Estonia was a new democratic state with a new market economy and had begun to implement agrarian reform in order to restore land to its former owners. This development had variable effects on nature protection measures and this gave rise to new conflicts.

At the same time Estonia had promoted tourism (there were 1.5 million foreign tourists in 1993 and the economic contribution of tourism was 8% of GNP and 13 %

of exports; 54,000 jobs were related to tourism, representing 8% of the workforce).

The development of Estonian tourism was centred largely on nature (7% of the territory is in protected areas, and there are 4 State nature reserves, 4 national parks, 1 biosphere reserve and 479 protected areas, including 13 landscape reserves). However, despite the existing conservation arrangements, new measures were required to protect the Estonian countryside.

Estonia's future "Environment Protection Strategy" included a special section on the protection of landscape diversity, with measures relating to tourism, such as:

-       consideration for tourism when devising management plans for protected areas;
-       provision to allocate receipts from tourism to the State budget for expenditure on nature protection;
-       steps to develop eco-tourism;
-       campaigns to promote nature as a special feature of Estonia.

Accordingly, an Estonian law on landscape protection was currently being prepared, with the prime objectives of:

-       creating the appropriate conditions for the preserving of human well-being and biodiversity by protecting the landscape and shaping its features;
-       conserving and enhancing the appearance, aesthetics and variety of characteristic landscapes through sustainable use.

5.3.3   A legal instrument for the protection of the French coast: the National Coastal Conservatory, by Louis BRIGAND (University of West Brittany, France)

In the course of the 20th century, coastal areas, which were once regarded as a hostile, inhospitable environment, had become a sought after and coveted site for a diverse range of competing and sometimes diametrically opposed activities. The rapporteur stressed that natural coastal habitats had been transformed to an amazing extent under the pressure of urban development.

Natural habitats on the coastline were extremely vulnerable from an ecological point of view and subjected increasingly to human pressure, especially tourism; this meant that, when managing and developing these sites, account should be taken of their environmental sensitivity and an assessment should be made of their capacity to cope with visitors.

Within a few decades tourism had become a major activity in coastal areas and the effects on natural habitats were directly linked with the prevailing type of tourism. The adverse effects of tourism - which could be calculated for example in terms of artificial development - had led to the introduction of new protection measures, particularly in the form of new legislation and the adoption of management plans designed to programme and plan the future of protected areas.

However, the major problem was still the dangers constituted by urban development, which could be combated most effectively by buying up areas of coastline which needed protection; this is what had motivated the recent acquisitions of coastal areas by local authorities who were able to raise the necessary funds for this purpose through a tax levied on all new building work.

This was also how the Coastal Conservatory had become involved.

The Conservatory was a public, state-run organisation set up under a law of 10 July 1975 to acquire natural sites threatened with damage or destruction and preserve their wealth and diversity for future generations; it had powers over coastal cantons and land owned by municipalities bordering on lakes or other stretches of water measuring over 1,000 hectares.

After 20 years in existence, the Conservatory owned 334 sites covering 44,334 hectares with 622 km of shoreline or 10% of the total length of the French coastline (the long-term objective was to acquire one third of the coastline); the Conservatory was run with the financial backing of the State but it could receive donations and legacies.

In conclusion to his talk, Mr BRIGAND mentioned the role that the Conservatory also played in providing scientific information and its duty to guarantee the quality of the sites it acquired; to carry out its tasks as effectively as possible the Conservatory pooled its resources with local authorities in respect both of acquisition programmes and of management plans and agreements.

Thanks to its experience in the acquisition and rehabilitation of coastal sites and in their development for tourist use, the Conservatory (like the National Trust in Great Britain) had become a role model for the sustainable protection and management of European coastal natural habitats.

5.3.4   Three reports on current projects:

-    In Ukraine (Mr Mikhail D. SYROTA - Environment Committee of the Parliament).

The principles of environmental protection were set out in the Constitution and therefore the Government and the Parliament were setting up an appropriate legislative system, having recently adopted a Tourism Act which took account of the environment;

-    In Albania (Mr. Genc METOHU, Architect, - Ministry of Construction and Tourism): a strategy for tourist development was currently being drawn up with the objective of making sustainable use of the natural resources offered by the still under-developed and under-populated Mediterranean coast; the strategy should cater for the new rights of private owners following land privatisation and regulate them as effectively as possible;

- in the "former Yugoslav Republic of Macedonia" (Ms Zorica SMILEVA - Ministry of the Economy), the Government was in the process of establishing an environmental policy including ecological monitoring and a tourist policy, based on the principles of sustainable development.

6. KEY IDEAS AND PARADOXES EMERGING FROM THE DISCUSSION

— Sustainable tourist development entails a new approach towards space and time:

- the long-term attraction of an area for tourists depends on its quality;

- sustainable development should not merely focus on short-term goals, but anticipate medium-term development and meet long-term requirements.

— Sustainable tourist development is based on the following principles:

- the intrinsic and irreplaceable value of nature;

- the acknowledgement that our heritage is a legacy which we receive and must pass on;

- individual and collective co-responsibility in the management of the natural and cultural heritage;

- natural solidarity between past, present and future generations, whose successive contributions and acts can enhance or destroy the common heritage.

— Sustainable tourist development enables a balance to be established between:

- the legitimate desire of tourist operators to make economic profits on the one hand;

- and tourist customers' expectations of quality on the other.

— Sustainable tourist development is a factor conducive to social cohesion:

- between the constituent members of the local population, assuming that their interests are taken into account in an overall approach towards implementing a development project;

- between local populations and tourists whenever there is contact between them.

— Sustainable tourist development contributes towards local democracy and training in citizenship:

- by attempting to devise an overall development policy which transcends individual interests in pursuit of an objective which is in the general interest;

18

- by involving private individuals in collective projects run by the local authorities;

- by providing training in the tourist professions focusing on quality;

- by educating and training tourist operators;

- by teaching tourist consumers;

- by encouraging people to change their behaviour and respect the area they are visiting.

— But paradoxes emerged which could no doubt be overcome by constantly seeking ways and means of establishing:

- a balance between the rights and the duties of citizens (individual rights of free access and the acceptance of restrictions in the general interest - the right to private property and the duty of co-responsibility for the collective natural or cultural heritage);

- a partnership between the private and public sectors (more suited to sustainable tourist development than systematic nationalisation programmes or privatisation across the board);

- solidarity between municipalities dealing with the same area;

- inter-regional and transfrontier co-operation for a shared future;

- a new social contract between country folk and city-dwellers for the enjoyment of their common natural and cultural heritage;

- a new quality of tourism, which lends itself to social communication and shared experience between visitors and local populations.

OPENING ADDRESS

Dr. Avraam LOUCA
Permanent Secretary, ministry of Agriculture,
Natural resources and Environment, Cyprus

It is a great pleasure for us to host in the Cyprus International Colloquy on Sustainable Tourism and the Environment which has been organized by the Council of Europe in co-operation with our Ministry of Agriculture, Natural Resources and Environment and the Tourism Organization.

On behalf of the Government and the people of Cyprus I would like to extend to you all a very warm welcome to Cyprus and wish this Colloquy every success.

As pointed out in the recent "Europe's Environment Report", the key elements for sustainable tourism are a longer-term perspective on policy-making, recognising the interdependence of economic and environmental systems and a concern for the biological limits within which human activities need to stay. In order to achieve all this, we need to balance social, cultural and environmental elements against economic parameters and tourism satisfaction. Above all, it is necessary to have an ocean of prudence.

The present Colloquy is a highly important event convened at a crucial point in time and in the right setting. One of the great challenges encountered by the countries represented here is the imperative necessity of the rational management of tourism development. In this respect it is important for policy-makers to take a closer look into those systems that have been successful and consider in detail the reasons for the drawbacks of other, as choices will have to be made between short-term needs and long-term sustainability. I believe that there is no better place to search for answers to this issue than in the Mediterranean Basin, which is the world's most important tourist destination, attracting some 35% of the international tourists world wide, and in a country with a long tourist tradition where tourist arrivals are forecasted to rise from 2 million in 1995 to between 3.3 - 5 million by the year 2005.

There is a broad consensus that tourism is very important for growth and can stimulate the development of other sectors. When tourism is well planned and managed and the relevant policy incorporates a serious concern for the environment, the industry can be sustainable. Otherwise, irrational tourism development entirely guided by market mechanisms and an absence of effective regulatory measures and efficient institutions, allow an unavoidable inherent tendency to arise which degrades the environment on which it largely depends for its continued well-being.

I need not dwell on the issue of the impact of tourism, neither on the fact that there has been a rapid decline in tourist levels in places where the industry had damaging effects on environments and cultures. Among others they have been amply highlighted in the relevant report prepared earlier this year under the auspices of the Steering Committee of the Conservation and Management of the Environment and Natural Resources of the Council of Europe.

Before concluding, allow me to say a few words about Cyprus, at the crossroads of three continents, with many physical and other attractions with convenient accessibility by sea and air, constitutes not only an ideal base for enterprises with business interests in the region, but also a fine tourist destination.

The island's advantages as an excellent place for tourism and business operations are enhanced by a healthy economy, a moderate cost of living, the high standard of professional services, good industrial relations and the minimum of Government bureaucracy.

The Government of Cyprus follows a liberal economic policy leaving development mainly in the field of private initiative but offering at the same time tax and other incentives and directing activity in the desired sectors of the economy. Hence, its policy is so designed as to encourage foreign participation, particularly joint ventures in order to attract not only foreign capital buy also advanced know-how in production and management.

In Cyprus, it cannot be denied that in the past we approached the tourism industry as though the environment had a infinite capacity to adjust to the pressures exerted upon it. The negative impacts were mostly caused by the need to speedily revitalize our economy, as a matter of national survival, immediately after the 1974 Turkish invasion which resulted in the occupation by the Turkish army of about 40% of our territory and in the loss of around 70% of our productive resources.

Today, most of the problems have been identified and a host of responsive and new proactive measures have been taken. Currently, our main objective is to slow down coastal development and enhance the quality of existing development, improve allocation of water resources and encourage more efficient water usage and protect our natural and cultural heritage. The most recent measures I can point out are the full implementation of the provision of the town and country planning legislation, the approval of the environmental management and control laws, to be further enhanced by framework laws on the environment and the protection of nature, the application of an environmental impact assessment system and the new regulatory policy on tourism. More importantly, proven workable links between environmental management, physical planning and tourism management frameworks and normative authorities have been the established.

The process of learning from positive and enlightened approaches will most certainly be assisted by this Colloquy and we are privileged that you have chosen to hold it in Larnaca. We are aware that we stand to benefit from your presence here and we share, of course, this benefit with all of you, a thought which makes us especially happy. It is in this spirit that we always actively support regional activities such as this one. I take this opportunity to express our sincere appreciation to the Council of Europe and the resource persons for organizing and facilitating the Colloquy and to Mrs Hélène Bouguessa, whose untiring efforts have made possible its realization.

Apart from the attractive beaches, the excellent hotel and the good wines, there are many other things to enjoy in Cyprus. The numerous and rich archaeological sites can meet and please any interest. The serenity of the mountains and its monasteries are not very far away. Above all, Cyprus is a place where the islanders greet you as one of their own with a natural spontaneous hospitality and friendliness that is too rarely found in most holiday destinations.

With these thoughts, I wish you every success in the Colloquy and to each and every one of you a pleasant stay on our island and a safe journey home.

THE COUNCIL OF EUROPE'S SPECIFIC ACTIVITIES
IN FAVOUR OF THE COUNTRIES OF
CENTRAL AND EASTERN EUROPE

Mrs Hélène BOUGUESSA
Environment Conservation and Management Division
Council of Europe, Strasbourg, France

First of all I wish to express the Council of Europe's warmest thanks to the Cypriot authorities for agreeing to host and organise this colloquy and for thus giving us the pleasure of meeting here on this magnificent island of Cyprus, a particularly appropriate venue for an event dealing with tourism and conservation of the natural environment.

I wish to thank in particular Dr Avraam Louca, Permanent Secretary and the other representatives of the Ministry of Agriculture, Natural Resources and the Environment and of the Cypriot tourism authority, with whom we liaised in preparing this event.

At this colloquy I have the honour of representing the Directorate of Environment and Local Authorities of the Council of Europe and I would first like to say a few words about this intergovernmental organisation, to which the Republic of Cyprus acceded as far back as 1961.

The Council of Europe was founded in 1949 to mark the healing of the breach between nations after the Second World War. Its headquarters were established in Strasbourg, a city on the border between Germany and France and a symbol of Franco-German reconciliation.

The organisation is based on the principles of defence of human rights and pluralist democracy, awareness among the citizens of Europe of their European cultural identity and identification of solutions to the problems of our society (examples are the combat against racism and xenophobia, cross-border co-operation, and - as this subject is of particular interest to us - environmental protection and the preservation of biodiversity).

The Council of Europe has thus been striving for over 45 years to build a united Europe, founded on the rule of law and on a joint response to the challenges confronting our societies.

In 1989 a further objective was added, that of developing a political partnership with the new democracies of Central and Eastern Europe and of helping these countries with their political, legislative and constitutional reforms. Since the political turning point of 1989 the Council of Europe has made a decisive contribution to the dissemination of democratic values and practices in Central and Eastern Europe. The

Berlin wall came down slightly more than five years ago, yet most of the new democracies of Central and Eastern Europe are already fully-fledged members of the Council while the others, including the European republics which emerged from the former Soviet Union, are striving to comply with the standards of democracy imposed as a condition for their accession.

The organisation therefore has 36 members at present, compared with 24 in 1989. The most recent arrivals are Albania and Moldova, which acceded in June 1995. Other Central and Eastern European States will follow in the near future, in particular the Russian Federation, which could become a member as from next year. The Council of Europe is destined to become the first Europe-wide political organisation.

It should be pointed out at this juncture that the Council of Europe's enlargement and opening up to the countries of Central and Eastern Europe did not pose any major identity problem for the organisation. In 1949 when its founders, including Winston Churchill, conceived the idea of setting up this sanctuary for Europe's democratic values and traditions of political pluralism and respect for the rule of law, the organisation was intended to encompass the entire continent. It became a purely West European institution as a result of the beginning of the Cold War and the emergence of the iron curtain. Hence, the collapse of the Berlin wall allowed the Council of Europe to spread to its natural extent, covering all of Europe, as in a revival of the European spirit of 1949.

Much of our activity is now focused on the pursuit of a strategy for Europe as a whole with the aim of creating a vast area of democratic security. The work done by the Council of Europe thus contributes to the common foreign and security policy to be implemented under the Treaty of Maastricht. In making this observation, I also wish to underline the complementary nature of the activities of the Council of Europe and the European Union, whose fifteen member States are of course part of our organisation.

The Council of Europe has entered into a deep-seated commitment vis-à-vis the countries of Central and Eastern Europe, whether or not they are members of the organisation, and is actively involved in training these countries for democracy and in implementing special assistance programmes.

These co-operation and assistance programmes in respect of the countries of Central and Eastern Europe constitute the Council of Europe's operational means of pursuing its policy of openness towards the new democracies, on the basis of the organisation's principles, values and attainments.

These programmes have a dual objective:

-        firstly strengthening, consolidating and accelerating the democratic reform process in these countries;

-       and secondly facilitating their gradual integration into the processes and structures of European co-operation, and of course first and foremost into the Council of Europe.

It follows from this dual objective that these programmes are primarily concerned with various aspects of the functioning of genuine pluralist democracies which are respectful of human rights and governed by the rule of law.

Nevertheless, this form of assistance likewise concerns all the other fields of activity coming within the Council of Europe's programme of work. Examples are the activities undertaken in the spheres of the Social Charter; the European Code of Social Security; equality between the sexes; the media; education, culture and sport; and protection of the environment.

The aim of this co-operation is to make member and non-member countries in Central and Eastern Europe ready to participate fully in the intergovernmental programme of activities. It also forms a multilateral framework within which the most developed Central and Eastern European countries can allow other countries in the region to benefit from their experience.

I wish to point out here that the activities proposed in the co-operation programmes are always a response to a request from the countries themselves, in that these countries identify their own needs and seek assistance, which they are always free to adapt or even to reject.

As regards to co-operation in the environmental field, which is of particular interest to us here, I have to say that this is unfortunately not a priority area and that the budget allocations fall far short of the needs. We have therefore had to make choices and have decided to concentrate on the sharing of experience and on training. However, we hope to develop the programme in future and to give more emphasis to technical assistance missions and specialist colloquies.

Since 1989 the co-operation programme in environmental matters has had two separate focuses:

-       legal co-operation with a view to adapting and amending legislation on nature conservation and environment protection in the wider sense; and

-       scientific and technical co-operation, principally through specialist colloquies, technical assistance and study visits to specialists in the various disciplines involved in the conservation of nature and biodiversity.

In the field of legal co-operation, I might cite the example of legislative assistance provided to various countries in preparing new laws governing water and air quality, regulating waste management or setting up protected areas. A model Law has also been prepared to help the countries of Central and Eastern Europe adapt their legislation. For instance, the Russian Federation drew inspiration from this text in drafting its new laws on the environment. Study visits to West European universities or legal institutes have also been organised for legal specialists and senior public officials responsible for implementing legislation.

As regards to scientific co-operation, two very different problems were tackled through technical assistance missions in 1995: techniques for use in cleaning up soil pollution in Poland and Bulgaria, and sustainable tourism development in Belarus, Slovakia and Albania.

In the case of technical assistance in setting up sustainable tourism development schemes, it is of particular interest to note that the study conducted in Belarus related to the opening-up to tourism of the Berezinski biosphere reserve in the North of the country. This is a huge area of land with an outstanding natural heritage, and for obvious economic reasons its managers want to open up these assets to controlled, reasonable tourism.

In Slovakia's case the study, part of which was carried out by our general rapporteur, Ms Suzanne Thibal, concerned two areas: the Danube region close to Bratislava, where rural tourism could be developed among other activities, and the mountainous Upper Tatras, which has significant potential as a year-round tourist region.

Lastly, the mission entrusted to us by Albania concerned a coastal region near Tirana intended for intensive tourism development, and we were asked to provide assistance with the assessment of tourism facilities already planned, the development of local agriculture oriented towards tourism and the creation of environmental education structures.

The specialist colloquies organised in the course of this year's programme were held on the following themes:

-       agriculture and related activities in protected areas - this colloquy was held in Russia during the first week of September and was organised in co-operation with the Russian Ministry of the Environment;

-       landscape protection in connection with sustainable development of forests, organised in Switzerland at the beginning of October with the Federal Forestry Department; and

-       a colloquy on environmental education held two weeks ago in Albania in the framework of the bilateral programme with this country.

After describing these activities it is natural to move on to the theme of tourism development, which we are gathered here to discuss. I shall not attempt to take the place of the specialists who will be speaking on this subject.

However, I would like to point out that the Council of Europe has been dealing with the issues raised by tourism since the seventies; this applies in particular to educational and cultural tourism, but is also true of aspects of tourism connected with mobility and freedom of movement, conservation of the architectural heritage and restoration of historical cities and towns, and the legal and social security problems engendered by tourism.

The Council of Europe has placed special emphasis on encouraging cultural tourism and has supported the creation of cultural routes such as the Silk Routes, the Baroque Routes and the routes devoted to the rural habitat and monasticism. The thinking behind these cultural routes is based on exchanges, sharing, mutual knowledge and discovery by European citizens of their common origins.

As regards tourism development and the environment, I would like to remind you that sustainable tourism was one of the themes examined at the pan-European ministerial conference on the environment, which recently took place in Sofia, Bulgaria, and which some of you attended. For those who were not present, I might point out that the conference in Sofia was the third of its kind and brought together on the theme of "An environment for Europe" ministerial-level representatives from all the States of Greater Europe, the United States and Canada, observers from OECD countries and representatives of major banks.

The Council of Europe had been asked to report to the conference on the subjects of a pan-European biological and landscape diversity strategy, co-ordination of environmental information, particularly concerning protected areas, and lastly tourism and the environment. At the end of its proceedings the conference approved the pan-European biological and landscape diversity strategy, which should constitute the reference framework for future work by the Council of Europe in the environmental field, in particular as regards sustainable tourism.

The report on tourism and the environment presented at the Sofia conference was drawn up by Mr Anthony Ellul, one of the rapporteurs at this colloquy. This report was prepared in the framework of a Council of Europe group of specialists chaired by Mr Patroclos Apostolides, representing. This group of specialists, which also includes Mrs Suzanne Thibal, was set up in 1993 and has issued a number of recommendations to governments, which are also available. The group will continue its standard-setting work next year and will also hold a colloquy in September or October on the theme of "Tourism and the environment: towards a new tourism culture". This colloquy will be hosted by Italy.

This brings us to the present colloquy in Larnaca, the purpose of which is to promote the sharing of experience among different countries of Europe and to pool ideas triggered by the development of tourism, whether in Western Europe, Central Europe or the Mediterranean Basin.

As you no doubt know, the countries on the shores of the Mediterranean are host to almost one third of international tourism and are probably the leading tourist region world-wide. This marvellous island of Cyprus is therefore an ideal venue for joint reflection on the advantages and disadvantages of tourism.

We are all in agreement that tourism is a very positive factor for modernisation and economic, social and cultural vitalisation. However, at the same time, poorly planned tourism has significant adverse, destabilising effects. Concentration of thousands of people in the same place at the same time can have a huge impact, in particular on the natural and cultural environment. The solution to this contradiction lies in a form of integrated, ecosystem-friendly tourism development, which makes use of natural resources without destroying them.

Conservation of natural resources is not a luxury for developed countries, but a vital necessity for the future, and the tourism industry must take account of this.

A further matter which should concern us is growth in the number of tourists and in ensuing pressure not only on the environment, but also on local people. The capacity to cater for tourists is not unlimited, and systems controlling and restricting tourism already exist in countries such as Austria. Pressure from tourism can but increase if containment measures are not introduced and if a balance is not struck between tourism needs and objectives and protection of the natural and cultural heritage.

The short-term lure of profits from large-scale tourism could lead to the destruction of resources and the loss of investments in the long term. In-depth cost-benefit analyses should also be carried out to ensure that local people reap the benefits of tourism. World Bank reports have shown that 55% of the revenue generated by tourism is lost to the host countries, and this figure may conceal much higher losses in less developed countries.

There can be no doubt that international tourism is a threat to the environment, but its consequences for the social and economic structures that have evolved over the centuries are also insufficiently known. The data cannot easily be discerned from industrial development studies, and it is no doubt necessary to establish new economic indicators taking account of social and environmental factors disregarded in the economic statistics. It is only by conducting special studies on the cultural, social and environmental effects of tourism that we will be able to obtain a truer picture of all of the opportunities and constraints inherent in the tourism industry.

After these brief considerations on tourism, I would like to come back to the values promoted by the Council of Europe - defence of human rights and individual freedoms, the fight against intolerance and xenophobia - and conclude by pointing out that there is a link between these values and sustainable tourism development. The link is an obvious one since tourism is conducive to exchanges, communication, reciprocal knowledge, dissemination of ideas and, let us hope, mutual respect.

TOURISM DEVELOPMENT POLICY AND
ENVIRONMENTAL PROTECTION IN CYPRUS

Patroclos A. APOSTOLIDES
Town Planner - Architect
Ministry for Agriculture, Natural Resources
and the Environment, Cyprus

A.   GENERAL

1.   Cyprus is the third largest island in the Mediterranean. It covers an area of 9,250 sq. km. and has a coastal length of 790 km. The main natural characteristics are the cental Mesaoria plain with Pentadaktylos range to the north and Troodos range to the southwest, with the highest point, chionistra, at an altitude of 1,960 m.

2.   The population of Cyprus numbers about 600 000 in the free areas. Since 1974 one- third of the island has been under military occupation. In the occupied areas, the census of the local population has been distorted by the presence of 40,000 troops and an equal number of settlers from Turkey. The largest part of the population is concentrated in the urban areas. Sixty-eight per cent (68%) live in Nicosia which is the capital, and in the Limassol, Larnaca and Pafos coastal urban centres. Thirty-two per cent (32%) live in rural areas in the hinterland.

3.   The Gross National Product in 1994 was CYP 3.5 billion. Earnings from tourism represent approximately forty-two per cent (42%) of the total revenue from the exportation of goods and services, while its contribution to the GNP is estimated at twenty-one (21%). Tourism offers employment - direct and indirect - to twenty-five per cent (25%) of the gainfully employed population (268,400). Foreign earnings are estimated at around CYP 810 million (1,380 million ECU) indicating that tourism is today the major earner of foreign income for the island.

4.   In 1994 there were 2,070,000 visitors to the island. In the decade 1980 - 1990 the number of visitors rose rapidly from 0.43 million to 1.56 million. Visitors to the island numbered 1.56 million in 1990, 1.39 million in 1991, 1.99 million in 1992, 1.84 million in 1993 and just over 2 million in 1994 due to both external factors and measures introduced by the Government.

5.   Eighty-six per cent (86%) of the total tourism on the island comes from European countries, of which approximately fifty-two per cent (52%) from the U.K. Other major countries of origin are Germany six per cent (6%), Sweden four per cent (4%), Greece three per cent (3%) and other Central and Eastern European countries. Outside Europe, four per cent (4%) come from Israel, two per cent (2%) from America, two per cent (2%) from Lebanon, two per cent (2%) from the Gulf, two per cent (2%) from the Middle East and the remainder from other countries.

31

6.   Today there are approximately 76,000 beds available in approved CTO accommodation (244 hotels, 270 hotel apartments and other types of accommodation). Of these, 71,000 beds are to be found in coastal areas. Thirty-eight per cent (38%) in the eastern areas of Protaras and Ayia, thirty-four per cent (34%) in the southern area of Larnaca and Limassol and twenty-three per cent (23%) to the west of Paphos.

7.   Given the generally pleasant climate with mild winters and warm summers, and three hundred days of sunshine yearly, tourism in Cyprus was mainly oriented towards sun, sea and sand. Over recent years however, there has been a notable turn towards alternative forms of tourism such as special interests, conventions, sport (especially in winter), cultural, rural (agrotourism), nature expeditions and bird watching, etc. all year round, reflecting the rich variety of natural attractions and assets available on the island.

8.   Tourism development is the responsibility of the Cyprus Tourism Organisation, a semi-Governmental Institution operating under the supervision of the Ministry of Commerce, Industry and Tourism. Co-operation is however established with other Ministries: the Ministry of Finance and the Planning Bureau for what concerns National Economic Planning; the Ministry of the Interior regarding Physical Planning (regional and local); the Ministry of Agriculture, Natural Resources and the Environment for general environmental considerations.

9.   Co-operation and the direct involvement of the local community is a pre-requisite for the implementation of planning decisions made on a local scale. Co-operation is also constant with the private sector where an active and positive participation in the development of tourism industry is widely acknowledged.

B.   PROBLEMS

10.   Tourism development in Cyprus following the post-invasion period, can be broken down into three stages:

11.   Stage I covers the period 1974-1981. A period of the Emergency Economic Plans. Following 1974, a year during which the existing tourism development stock and infrastructure were lost to the occupation forces, a massive effort was undertaken by the Government to reinstate the Cypriot Economy, tourism in particular.

12.   Objectives to this end were, among others:

a.   the reinstatement of Cyprus on the world tourist map,
b.   planning in order to create extra beds for tourists,
c.   the creation of related infrastructure,
d.   the development of international tourism,
e.   the co-ordination of tourism with other general development plans,
f.   the extension of the tourist season, etc.

13.   While the targets at the time were essentially economic in nature, it was clear that environmental considerations were of crucial importance for sustainable development in the future. Beach capacity, social contact ratios and environmental protection enhancement were the adopted terms in the formulation of tourism development policies and programmes. This is the characteristic of Stage II, which covers the period 1982 to 1990.

14.   Stage II

        During this period the growth rate of tourism remained constantly high, averaging between 20-22% per annum in spite of the measures taken, the incentives introduced and the legal and fiscal means of control enacted.

15.   The rapid rate of growth characteristic of this period brought with it a number of adverse affects, i.e.:

a.   massive structures erected along the coast obstructing the visual contact and functional relationship between the sea and the hinterland (high densities, high rise, structures very close to the sea),

b.   Hindered accessibility (both vehicular and pedestrian) to the beach due to the continuous boundaries of land ownership,

c.   Lack of open spaces for public use, especially along the coast,

d.   Overcrowding phenomena along certain beaches (Ayia Napa, Protaras) with social contact ratios reaching over-saturation levels, especially during the peak season, aggravated by the influx of weekenders from other parts of the island (Nicosia),

e.   Constant rise of the price of land as a result of high demand and the limited availability of suitable coastal land,

f.   Loss of fertile agricultural land to tourism (Famagusta, Paphos). Similarly conflict in land use between industrial development and tourism,

g.   Coastal erosion due to the proximity of buildings to the waterfront (Limassol Larnaca) and as a result of river damming in the hinterland,

h.   Excessive pressure on resources. Shortages in water supply, especially during a period of low rainfall, and in the labour force, both due to the ever-increasing demands made by the tourism sector

i.   Air, water, ground and noise pollution, through inadequate disposal of sewage and waste material, heavy traffic both on land and in the sea (pleasure boats), misuse of loudspeakers, etc.

j.   Structures (wave-breakers) on the coast either to protect the coast from erosion or to create additional beach areas to accommodate more people, resulted in visual disfigurement of the coast, and in certain cases, distorted the ecosystem of the coastal area,

k.   Spoiling of the purity of the landscape and environmental degradation stemming from the need to construct new motorways and other roads. Aggravation of traffic problems, negative visual impact on nature, due to the many signs erected, traffic signs or for advertising purposes (goods and places to visit),

l.   Pressures for further development and land exploitation within and around historic sites and antiques as land is mostly privately owned. Conflict concerning land use around historic sites and the disfigurement of these sites by new structures erected on adjoining land. Lack of adequate funds to acquire land in order to protect it, aggravated the problem,

m.   Changes in social customs and traditions of local people because of the influence of the customs of the visitors arriving in large numbers. In Ayia Napa, for example, social contact ratio (locals/tourists) is about 1:14 during peak season,

n.   Destruction of architectural heritage in villages owing to hasty reconstruction without due care given to the character and traditional values of the structure,

o.   Ageing and diminishing of the rural population. Young people are attracted to the coastal urban developments by the job opportunities generated by tourism. At the same time, the urbanisation process is expedited.

16.   At the same time, certain positive effects are noted:

a.   The income generated by tourism enables local authorities to invest in projects which are necessary to the residents' welfare,

b.   The revitalization of traditional arts and crafts. Villages otherwise remote or unknown become centres of interest and attraction,

c.   A general improvement in the standard of living,

d.   Enhancement of cultural activities (folkloric dancing, music, etc.),

e.   Diversification in employment opportunities,

f.   Enriched experiences through contact with visitors from different cultural backgrounds.

17.   During this period, the lack of infrastructure and services, the excessive pressure on resources, water and labour in particular, the destruction of the environment and in many cases the quality of life, pollution in all possible forms and above all, the realisation of the absence of a meaningful environmental policy, have had a strong impact in the formulation of development policies for the future.

18.   It has also been acknowledged that a growing environmental awareness among the public and the need for a wider participation in the formulation of the tourism development strategy, as well as the need for protective measures to address the environmentally sensitive or vulnerable areas, were of paramount importance.   In addition, it was realised that diversification and enrichment of the tourist product was necessary so that pressure on coastal areas be alleviated and the interest of tourists be directed to other areas of the island or sectors of tourism.

19.   To a considerable extent the greater part of Cyprus' environmental problems are attributable, albeit indirectly, to past macro-economic policies. Such policies have been biased against environmental considerations and characterised by protectionism and distorted resource valuation, thereby discouraging "environmentally friendly" behaviour by the public and private sectors. Excess waste and inefficient use of resources can be linked to inappropriate pricing and subsidisation. Effective lobbying efforts on the part of developers, farmers, etc. have also contributed to a pattern which overlooked degradation of resources.

20.   By 1989, however, it was more than clear that the environmental problems were pressing and a growing awareness among the people necessitated the introduction of drastic measures and policies to deal with them. It was more than acknowledged that growth in numbers was not associated with adequate provision and improvement in facilities and services, and it was therefore important that quantity be accompanied by quality in the tourist product. Diversification of the economy was also necessary to alleviate the heavy dependence on tourism.

21.   Thus June 1989 marks the beginning of Stage III, with the enactment of the Moratorium on tourism development in all coastal areas in order to allow for the time needed for the preparation of a National Tourism Development Policy.

22.   Following this, the following major actions were taken by the Government in November 1990:

a.   the enactment of the Town and Country Planning Law, and
b.   the introduction of the new Tourism Development Policy.

23.   With the Town and Country Planning Legislation environmental issues were afforded high priorities. Planning is promoted on three levels, National, Regional and Local. Local Plans, area development schemes and the declaration of rural development policy are currently the instruments in force. A planning permit is a pre-requisite to all forms of development, and therefore no development could take place without a permit. Tourism development is an integrated part of the overall development programme of the

island, all coastal areas, areas of natural beauty, site and buildings of historic or cultural heritage are adequately protected and finally participation by the public in the decision-making process for the preparation of development plans is safeguarded. Environmental impact assessment studies must be prepared for all major development projects, including tourist projects. Measures to protect environmentally sensitive areas have been implemented. Three major areas have already been declared "National Parks" (Akamas, Troodos and Cavo Greco forests) and other areas are under consideration to the same end.

24.   The new Tourism Development Policy also acknowledges the need for the protection and enhancement of the environment (natural, cultural, social). Stricter control on tourism development in coastal areas, at a distance of 3 km. from the shore, was enforced. The main aim being to discourage and slow down rates of tourism development, while at the same time any new project would demonstrate environmental quality and enhanced services. Minimum site requirements were specified to ensure the harmonisation of new development with its surroundings and the natural environment in general. Programmes for the promotion of alternative forms of tourism and diversification of tourism in other (non-coastal) parts of the islands were introduced.

25.   Tourism, more than any other activity, depends primarily on quality human and natural environment and resources. In its manifestation though, it is characterised by fast short-term development which, in many cases, damages those very assets it seeks to promote. If it is not to contribute to environmental degradation and destroy itself in the process, the tourism industry, like other economic activities, must recognise its responsibility to the environment and vulnerability to over-exploitation and learn how to become sustainable.

26.   Sustainable development advocates leaving no less of the stock of natural resources inherited from previous generations, to future generations. This implies preventing irreversible damage to environmental assets which have no substitute and prevent such hazards as pollution, solid and beach erosion, destruction of ecosystems, cultural and social values, etc.

27.   Sustainable tourism development calls for a set of development policies and strategies with due respect and without detriment to the environment, the resources (natural, cultural) and quality of life on which continued human activity and further development (economic and social) depend. At the same time, it meets the needs of the present without compromising the ability of future generations to meet their own needs.

28.   Sustainable tourism seeks harmony between the basic objectives which are inherent to any tourism development in order to meet the needs and the creative right of future generations. These objectives being:

a.   economic wealth,
b.   subjective well-being,
c.   optimum satisfaction of guest requirements,
d.   healthy culture,
e.   protection of resources and conservation of nature.

29.   In general, sustainable tourism refers to any form of tourist development or activity which:

-       respects the environment
-       ensures long-term conservation of natural and cultural resources
-       is socially and economically acceptable and equitable.

30.   In considering sustainable development it is necessary to refer to and resolve the conflict between two schools of thought:

-       the development oriented approach
-       the ecologically oriented approach

31.   The supporters of the development approach view sustainability as a concept supporting man-made construction which enhances the value of the environment. They propose extensive usage of the environment just as long as the aggregate value of both natural and man-made capital grows with time.

32.   On the other hand, the ecological approach stresses the irreversible damage of development on the natural environment, and questions the appropriateness of human activity in certain ecosystems. It maintains that certain unique and fragile environmental systems should be designated as "prohibited" to all visitors.

33.   The concept of sustainability has been enjoying increasing attention in the last few years due to the growing public awareness of environmental issues. Indicative of the special consideration it receives, the United Nations Conference on the Environment and Development, held its "Earth Summit" in Rio de Janeiro in June 1992. In the spirit of this Summit, sustainable tourism covers all forms and destinations, mass tourism and small scale travel, cities and rural areas. A small proportion of the industry as a whole consists of "nature-based" tourism which encompasses both nature tourism and ecotourism.

34.   The priority and significance which is afforded on the need for sustainable development is also reflected in a very recent document, the draft recommendation on a general policy for a sustainable and environmentally friendly tourism development, issued by the Committee of Ministers of the Council of Europe to Governments of Member States, which was approved in September 1994.

35.   Cyprus, as already mentioned, is promoting the necessary adjustments in incorporating this concept in the formulation of development policies.

36.   It has already been established that tourism development in Cyprus is essentially sun, sea and sand oriented. The negative impacts of the pressures exercised on the coast have already been identified. In order to alleviate pressure in coastal areas and respond more positively to environmental criteria within the concept of "sustainability", the efforts in the tourism development policy were directed towards enrichment and diversification of the tourist product. Indeed, this is the goal for the future. These new forms of tourism are promoted in order to satisfy the additional

needs and interests of the visitor and take advantage of assets of the Cypriot nature or culture.

37.   In this context, a major effort is being directed towards rural development, "agrotourism" in particular. By rural development we mean "any tourist activity which takes place in the rural environment".

38.   The term "agrotourism" as interpreted in Cyprus implies the development of villages through measures of revitalising and enhancing village life.

39.   Agrotourism development and promotion Cyprus is two-fold. First to reinstate and enhance public spaces or of buildings within a village for public use and second to reconstruct and put into profitable uses, compatible with rural life, private properties.

40.   A major programme on agrotourism has been undertaken by the Cyprus Tourism Organisation since 1991. This programme refers to a number of selected villages within which special architectural studies are undertaken with the aim of identifying public buildings or public areas significant to the identity of each village. These elements when restored and enhanced will add to the attractiveness of the village and serve as examples for similar actions by the private sector. Fiscal incentives are also offered to owners of private houses to improve and put them to some tourist use. The goal of the programme, which is part of a wider programme for rural development involving other Government departments, is to instal life in the villages and arrest urbanisation.

41.   "Ecotourism", a narrower concept of "nature tourism", is an additional aspect of rural tourism promoted in Cyprus. In spite of the small number of nature tourists and even smaller number of ecotourists, this type of tourist activity is steadily growing. Although ecotourism implies nature conservation and is usually practised by small groups of visitors, nature tourism has a wider meaning, in that simply people visit areas of natural interest and beauty. The latter however may take place in the form of pleasure trips which may not be ecologically sustainable. Vehicles used, or large numbers of visitors may cause irreparable damage to the resource.

42.   Ecotourists go to natural areas which are relatively untouched, with the specific aim to admire, study and enjoy the countryside and its plants and animals, and similarly to appreciate the past and present cultural characteristics of the areas visited. It is an activity, planned and carried out with environmental and social awareness. Finally, it is an economic process in which the concept of sustainability of natural resources is of primary consideration. Ecotourists participating in bird watching has been on the increase in Cyprus over the past few years.

43.   To facilitate nature tourism in Cyprus, measures have been taken to:

a.   identify and protect areas of natural beauty and incorporate them in National Parks and other protected areas,

b.   provide for nature trails with proper information systems on the content, nature, fauna and flora and historical aspects of the findings along the trail,

c.   indicate on maps the places of interest which are accessible through the open countryside,

d.   confine building activities or any form of human intervention to the absolute minimum and with due respect to the environmental quality and characteristics of each areas.

44.   Special interests tourism refers to the particular interests or abilities of each visitor or groups of visitors:

a.   Cultural tourism which implies among others archaeological interest. Visits therefore of archaeological or historic museums or archaeological or historic sites, are promoted. Cyprus, an island with rich historical background is one of the main attractions to people of special interests of this kind.

b.   Conventions and conference tourism is a fast growing sector of the tourist industry. Facilities to serve the needs of this segment of visitors have been provided by both the public and the private sectors. Most upper class hotels offer adequate facilities and means to meet convention needs. The International Conference Centre in Nicosia is the most significant one.

c.   Sports tourism is encouraged through the availability of playing fields in tourist areas. Sport activities is promoted as one of the basic factors for seasonality in tourism as many teams find winter in Cyprus quite warm as compared to winter conditions in their home countries.

d.   Golf in Cyprus is a relatively new field of activity. The first golf course in the Paphos area was completed last year and a second one is under construction. Both comply with international competition standards. Several other cases of active interest of investors in golf course development are under consideration. The programme envisages the development of a total of six golf courses on the island.

e.   The development of nautical tourism is also a major target of the policy for diversification of tourist activities in Cyprus. At present, there are two marinas operating in Cyprus. One at Larnaca, which is run by CTO, and one in Limassol which is privately owned. A new programme for the expansion of marinas has been approved by the Government this year and three additional marinas, two in Famagusta and one in Paphos coastal region of a total capacity of three thousand (3,000) berths will be constructed. The programme envisages the creation of marinas of various capacities and service potential at appropriate locations so that a full network of nautical facilities will be provided along the entire coastline.

f.   Finally, the creation of centres for studies or information are under consideration. In their primary form they are places where leaflets and other information is made available to the visitor. In a more organised form the centre may take the form of Ecomuseums where exhibitions, lectures and printed information may elaborate on ecological issues. Such centres may offer services to small groups or individuals with specials interests, groups of visitors in a general sense or provide for instruction on the protection of the environment or nature and cultural heritage.

45.   In concluding this paper, I will recognise that tourism is undoubtedly the backbone of development in Cyprus. Planning for tourism development in a sustainable and environmentally friendly manner is of paramount importance. Quality of life and richness should be ensured to both visitors and local people. Consciousness and sensitivity must be the characteristics of our actions.

46.   It is clear from the above that it is only through radical changes and adjustments in our way of thinking, immediate adjustments in manipulating growth and re-evaluation of our priorities, the pre-requisite for all development, the physical environment, both the natural and man-made could be effectively protected and enhanced to the benefit of all the people. It is our duty to respond to this challenge in the most positive and creative manner.

PLANNING FOR TOURISM IN THE FIELDS OF URBAN AND REGIONAL DEVELOPMENT AND ENVIRONMENTAL PROTECTION

Ermis KLOKKARIS
Architect and town planner
Town and Country Planning Department, Cyprus

SUSTAINABLE TOURIST DEVELOPMENT AND ISLAND SYSTEMS

Tourism, often regarded as a driving force for development, tends, if over-exploited, to threaten the very environment and culture on which it is founded. This raises the two main concepts discussed here, "development", in its broad sense, and "sustainability".

By "development" we mean progress, in the economic and technological sense but especially in the social sense and in terms of values. In a way, it is human development, a process of social equity which aims, among other things, to redistribute resources more fairly.

The equally widespread concept of "sustainability" implies the rational management of natural and cultural resources so that they may continue to be available for future generations.

"Sustainability" is a process, a comprehensive development policy that preserves the heritage and is of benefit to the population as a whole. In this sense, the concept of sustainability applied to tourism presupposes the lasting reconciling of development with protection of the natural and cultural heritage. It can also be seen as the type of development capable of satisfying the needs of both today's tourists and the host regions without restricting their opportunities for the future.

Lastly, it is a concept with three objectives:

- environmental balance and limitation of tourist numbers;
- alleviation of problems in areas already-developed;
- diversification of tourist "products" and promotion of new forms of integrated and specialised tourism.

Sustainable tourist development in the case of islands, however, becomes a rather difficult task because of problems of small scale, isolation, insular endemism and the strong social identity of groups. All these are aspects of the fragility of a system that is vulnerable to external pressures such as mass tourism.

Where island systems in general are concerned, at least in the field of regional planning under discussion here, reference is made especially to the mode of island development, the basis for the distribution of human settlements, traditional methods of exploiting natural resources and the cohesion and balance among all those aspects. The interpretation of existing land use illustrates man's close links with the sea (human beings prefer to settle in coastal areas), the preponderance of agricultural activity and the supportive and transitional roles played by the hinterland. This form of spatial organisation tends to give way, in the face of tourist over-development of islands, to coastal urbanisation, the decline of farming and a dwindling local population.

THE CASE OF CYPRUS

Cyprus is the third largest of the Mediterranean islands, after Sicily and Sardinia, with an area of 9,250km² and 782km of coastline. Consisting of two mountain ranges on either side of the broad Mesaoria Plain, the island is easily accessible. In 1993, Cyprus had a population of 722,800 inhabitants, only 32% of whom lived in rural areas.

Unfortunately the de facto division of the island and the occupation of 37% of its territory since 1974 by Turkish armed forces paints a different picture. This has meant that 82% of the population living in the southern part of the island (62% of the territory) have gravitated towards the 38% of coastline still under State control.

Until 1974 and for a long period afterwards, public planning policies encouraged tourist development, in order either to stimulate growth or to assist in economic recovery. Since then, tourism has been regarded as a growth industry and has gradually become the country's leading economic sector.

It was not until December 1990 that the Cypriot government introduced its official tourist policy and a physical, urban and rural planning system, pursuant to the Hotels and Tourist Establishments Law and the Town and Country Planning Law. These two instruments, together with the existing Streets and Buildings Regulation Law now form the legislative framework for tourist development.

Before discussing the specific provisions of the Urban Development and Regional Planning Act of interest here, a few words should be said about the "indicative economic planning" pursued since the 1960s, once the island had become independent, by the **Planning Bureau**, seeking to invest in the dynamism of the private sector and the power of the free market. The aim of the Five-year Plans, the five Special Economic Action Plans and the Strategic Development Plans already applied was to improve coordination of public investments, programme the State's capital expenditure and guide market choices in various fields, including tourism. Among the projects carried out were major water management and improvement schemes (dams, irrigation schemes, pipelines. etc).

With regard to the tourist policy introduced in 1990 by the Cyprus Tourism Organisation, you will have understood from the paper given by my colleague from the

42

Tourist Board that it consists of a set of regulations designed to control, more particularly in coastal areas, the provision and geographical distribution of tourist facilities and improve the quality and diversity of the "product". The most restrictive of the provisions is the one setting a minimum surface area for land to be developed for tourism.

The provisions of the Town and Country Planning Law are broader in scope, covering environmental protection and conservation as well as the physical and functional integration of tourism according to a well-defined siting strategy.

Where the environment is concerned and in the absence of any overall legislation in the field, it can be said that the Town and Country Planning Law is the chief instrument for the physical conservation and protection of nature. The provisions of the Act relating to the environment are the following :

- the rather broad interpretation given to the word "development" for which planning permission is required (i.e. any construction or demolition operation as well as any change in the activity for which a property is used);

- the definition of protected areas of environmental interest and the adoption of measures to restrict the use of such areas and construction within them. The same principle applies to the protection of farmland and forests;

- the introduction of environmental protection and integration criteria for building licences, to be fulfilled while the project is being carried out;

- the definition of "white" zones that may not be built upon for a fixed period of time, pending a concerted urban planning document;

- controls on the scope and location of any potentially harmful installation or activity (livestock rearing, industry, mines, quarries, etc) and the obligation to carry out impact assessment and/or site restoration;

- the conservation of a building or group of buildings or a site of architectural, historical or social interest or of natural beauty, and the protection of trees;

- the possibility of refusing or terminating the activity, or refusing the change of activity, for which a property is used; this may include the obligation to remove existing buildings;

- the introduction of a tourist planning policy which controls tourist development particularly outside tourist areas and urban development areas.

The Act provides for three types of plan governing, *inter alia*, tourist development:

- Country Site Policy,
- Local Plans,
- Area schemes.

Some aspects of these plans relating to tourist development are of particular interest here. The country site policy, which is similar to the National Urban Planning Regulations, replaces the "Island Plan" initially provided for in the Act and consists of a regulatory instrument and a zoning plan for each municipality for which a local plan does not yet exist. Each local plan, which is an urban development document presented in graphic and written form, covers one urban centre on the island.

The provisions of these first two types of plan differ depending on whether they refer to the coastal strip, which is three kilometres wide, or the inland region. They govern tourist development :

- essentially in tourist zones, defining land-use and extent of building (plot ratio, building height, built area of the plot);

- exceptionally in urban centres, in the form of a hotel, to enhance the function of town centres and to serve a different clientele;

- in urban development zones of the few rural communities, in the form of small, family tourist units, so as not to alter the scale and fabric of traditional village life and to make better use of the local workforce;

- selectively in rural areas, provided that the proposed tourist complex is multi-purpose and autonomous, respects the environment, supplements the region's technical and social infrastructure and enhances the existing product.

Further inland, tourist establishments are mainly authorised in Urban Development zones although a few multi-purpose, autonomous tourist complexes and a few isolated hotels in highland or upland areas may be authorised provided that they are justified.

These plans therefore contribute to consolidating urban areas, reinforcing the function of municipalities and maintaining their size, improving the spatial distribution of tourist installations and ensuring the supply of the necessary, related tourist services and infrastructure.

The Area-Specific Plans prepared by the Department of Town Planning and Housing for all tourist zones constitute the third physical planning level. The purpose of these basic schemes is to restructure tourist areas and improve the integration of buildings, by :

- defining the density, type and form of acceptable tourist installations;

- planning a graded road system, including footpaths, cycle paths and access roads or paths to the sea;

- providing a functional system of green areas and links between them;

- favouring low-density grouped development, which is one of the tourist policy's aims;

- proposing measures for the consolidation and extension of the coastal protection zone.

ASSESSMENT

Only partial conclusions can be drawn from all this since, in addition to the planning system that needs to be assessed, there are the insurmountable repercussions of the split in the country, which are too far-reaching for us to assess. What are the practical effects of this split which has severely disrupted the spatial organisation of Cyprus?

- The usual definition of the word "island" is called into question completely since Cyprus is no longer an island, given that it has a non-maritime border.

- The balance and unity of the island system is shattered since the island, split as it is in two, turns its back on its hinterland which becomes a *cul de sac* as a result.

- This bipolar means that infrastructure and services (roads, ports, airports, etc) have to be duplicated in a reduced, fragile territory.

- The introduction of borders, where there should not be any, in the sectors of the environment, natural resources and environmental disasters makes those sectors difficult to manage.

- The economic viability of an island state is largely compromised because of the rise of a services sector essentially dependent on foreign markets (example of tourism).

- The close relationship between inhabitants and habitat and the concept of "native soil" become meaningless in the case of an uprooted refugee population (identity crisis and severing of community links).

- Other consequences include the profound transformation of the land to fit an imported tourist stereotype, the inordinate expansion of towns, which are approaching the scale of continental towns, and the consumption of the environment, used merely as a means to economic growth.

45

In addition to the consequences of the split, there are also shortcomings in the island's planning tools:

- The absence of a strategic development document, such as the Island Plan originally provided for, prevents overall planning and consideration of the entire national territory.

- The absence of institutional means of inter-municipal and inter-agency cooperation makes the coordination of tourist development difficult.

- The provisions of the tourist policy and those of urban development documents sometimes overlap but are sometimes contradictory because of their differing goals.

What has been learnt, however, in the five years that these two instruments have been in application?

- The growth rate in the number of tourist beds has been very effectively controlled.

- The provisions of the Urban Development Act relating to the environment have contributed to the protection of some natural areas threatened by expanding tourism and to greater consideration of nature-related criteria.

- The absence of a regional planning dimension has widened regional disparities and has meant that the island's assets have not been wisely exploited.

- As most of the coastline has been designated as tourist area, commitments have been made to property owners, which cannot be ignored.

- The absence of effective tools for diverting investments towards new types of products has meant little diversification of supply and poor consideration of inland areas.

- The size and shape of the buildings are ill-suited to the small villages and the type of tourist installations planned have not always corresponded to clients' expectations.

- The introduction of measures controlling the geometry and dimensions of buildings and the difficulties raised regarding their appearance have posed problems for their physical integration.

- The absence of tax incentives in the field of environmental management (to compensate for environmental impairment, to obtain a building licence in an already developed area, etc) has demonstrated the ineffectiveness of physical measures alone.

All these assessment points reveal firstly that in the case of Cyprus the principles of sustainable development cannot be entirely respected, at least in the short- or medium-term, because of its divided territory.

However, the achievements since the introduction of the two planning instruments mentioned have been considerable, although it must be borne in mind that this is a long-term process.

The three objectives of sustainable tourist development (quantity-control, organisation and equipping of tourist areas, and product diversity) are gradually being attained.

Measures still need to be taken, however, in the fields of regional planning, design of new products, local development schemes, tax incentives, and rehabilitation of developed zones using area schemes.

THE SENSITIVE BALANCE:
NATURE PROTECTION - TOURISM - LOCAL COMMUNITY

CASE STUDY FROM NORTH-EASTERN HUNGARY

Janos LERNER
Aggtelek National Park, Hungary

1.   Introduction to the area

The Aggtelek National Park was established in 1985 on nearly 20,000 hectares in the territory of an earlier nature protection area. The area was declared a MAB Biosphere Reserve in early 1979. Nearly 1500 species of plant life (of which 106 are protected including the endemic Tornaian yellowdrop, registered in the Work Red Data Book), 42 species of fish, 13 species of amphibian, 9 species of reptiles, 178 species of birds (127 of whom nestle) and 27 species of mammal have been identified to date. The avifauna includes 23 species that are under threat in Europe (e.g. the Imperial Eagle, Rock Bunting) and require special protection.

The underground world also requires special attention as the caves, due to their genetic heritage, their characteristics, their colour and the shape of the stalagmites, demand a high level of protection. Twenty caves in the area are subject to special protection. The landscape is typically karstic and underground there are some 240 caves (in Hungary all the caves are protected by governmental decree). Caves attract many visitors for aesthetic, scientific and medical reasons, also those with a sense of adventure. The environmental conditions in the caves are good, with a constant temperature of 10°C in both summer and winter with high levels of steam (90-95%). The show-caves respect the required safety standards. The largest cave is Baradia-Domica with a total length of 25 kms and has three entrances on the Hungarian side; a variety of guided tours are offered.

Two villages can be found inside the park (1000 inhabitants), twelve others are just along the boundaries. The nearest industrial area is 60 kms away. Due to the favourable wind direction and the local hydrographic structure, no serious environmental damage can be expected.

2.   Present situation as seen from different points of view

NATIONAL PARK

-       The need for protection requires certain restrictions: e.g. regulations in grazing, forestry work, land cultivation, use of chemicals in fields. It is forbidden to enter the core areas of the biosphere reserve.

TOURISM

- 200,000 visitors a year → impact is concentrated around the cave entrances (litter, damage to grass) and in some areas inside (broken stalactites, handprints on stalagmites, growth of flora due to the artificial light). Tourist trails come close to the core areas (Blue trail).

LOCAL COMMUNITY

- Traditions (cattle grazing, charcoal burning, lime kilning, pottery, copper, woodcarving)

- Jobs (working in the national park as rangers, tour guides, maintenance, administration)

3.   For and against - battle of interests - needs/arguments

3.1   NATURAL ENVIRONMENT (sensitivity, vulnerability)

- caves → visitors
  - income for national parks
  - impact on environment

- forests, meadows → local people
  - utilization
  - destruction

3.2   NATIONAL PARK → PROTECTION → RESTRICTIONS

- for local community
- for visitors

(The task of the Government is to preserve the value of the area, vulnerable environment, endangered species, conservation)

3.3   VISITORS → ATTRACTION (recreation, relaxation, enjoyment)

3.4   LOCAL PEOPLE → TRADITIONAL UTILIZATION
(cultivation, forestry, survival)

4.   Task: find a balance → necessary compromise

Do needs and interests meet? Where and how? → Balance point

- Natural environment → Attraction for tourism/National Park's interest
- Local traditions → Attraction for tourism/Local's interest

Who is the appropriate organization to keep the balance?

-       National Park Authority → Combines the interests of nature protection, tourism
        and the locals

5.   Conclusions

The maintenance and preservation of the balance of nature protection, tourism and the local community is of primary importance. *Balance means to create a compromise between the needs and interests of nature protection, tourists and the local communities.*

National parks and Nature Conservation Authorities have to play a primary role in this activity as they are the only organization in a position to combine the interests of the three parties.

CO-OPERATION IN THE FIELD OF TOURISM AND MEDITERRANEAN CONFERENCES ON THE DEVELOPMENT OF SUSTAINABLE TOURISM

Robert LANQUAR
Professor and international consultant,
Co-ordinator and Rapporteur for the Ministerial Conferences
on Mediterranean Tourism, France

Tourism is being increasingly used in international co-operation as a tool for promoting the development of the Mediterranean region as a solution to both the decline in traditional Mediterranean agricultural activities and the problems of transforming industrial dockland areas and developing the services sector. This is the objective of international bodies in assisting the development of tourism.

a.   The European Union

The European Union has long been active in this field and has developed two main approaches: direct action in the Mediterranean regions of EU member countries, and special co-operation with other Mediterranean countries. The Commission has proposed more intensive dialogue on all questions of interest to both parties, in addition to the more specific questions of co-operation in the fields of trade and finance.

As a result of the support given by the European Community, these activities have really become a joint venture. A general framework was provided by the new Mediterranean Policy (1992-1996) which brings the Community's activities into line with the efforts made by the countries concerned, firstly in respect of their economic development (where the activities entail, for example, the implementation of economic reforms, the modernisation of economic management methods and the development of productive employment), and secondly with regard to their social development (where the activities entail, for example, the development of human resources, the reinforcement of institutions, the formulation and implementation of demographic policies). The new Mediterranean Policy gives priority to environmental protection: the survival of the land-locked Mediterranean, the future of fishing in its waters and of tourism, i.e. two indispensable activities for employment in the region, are at stake. It is, therefore, not surprising that there have already been many multilateral and Community actions designed to protect the Mediterranean Basin. However, no matter how much funding is made available for the various schemes it will always be insufficient in relation to the enormous financial requirements (30 billion ECU) which Mediterranean countries will have to meet in the near future.

Under the first series of activities, which took place between 1986 and 1992 with the integrated Mediterranean programmes (IMP), funds allocated to Italy, France and Greece with a view to adapting their economies to the accession of Spain and Portugal to the Community: 600 million ECU were earmarked for the adjustments in the tourist industry.

However, the most important schemes took place within the framework of Community structural funds, ERDF, EAGGF and the European Social Fund. These were reinforced by the introduction of the new Cohesion Fund. Since the reform of the structural funds, the main objective (Objective 1) now concerns underdeveloped regions (the Mediterranean coast and islands) - 1.7 billion ECU were allocated to tourism between 1989 and 1993. Contributions have also been allocated to other objectives of the structural funds such as Objective 5b for the promotion of rural tourism (180 million ECU) in France, Italy, Spain and Portugal during the same period).

A number of programmes, schemes and EC campaigns had a direct impact on tourism in the Mediterranean countries of the European Community:

- MEDSPA, 39 million ECU for environmental conservation;
- ENVIREG, 500 million ECU to promote tourism not detrimental to the environment;
- REGIS, 200 million ECU allocated to rural areas;
- LIFE, 400 million ECU for sustainable development.

Although not specifically aimed at Mediterranean countries, other EC campaigns concerning tourism have had an impact on the sustainable development and the environment of the region:

- training programmes such as COMETT, ERASMUS, PETRA, EUROTECNET, SKILL NEEDS;
- EC transport programmes, the gradual deregulation , on a step-by-step basis, of air transport and the extension of the network of high-speed trains;
- development of data processing in the tourist industry (ATIS and ULYSSES projects);
- tourism statistics pursuant to the decision of the Council of Ministers of 1990;
- subsidies for co-operation projects in favour of developing countries (only 5.4 million ECU) between 1976 and 1993;
- financing of tourist amenities and the modernisation of hotel infrastructures through the European Investment Bank;
- backing given to Operation Blue Flag set up by the Foundation for Environmental Education in Europe (information source on the quality of bathing water and beaches and incitement to improve them)

b.   The World Tourism Organisation

Although the Mediterranean countries co-operate within the WTO in three different regional committees (Europe, Africa and the Middle East), the organisation also intervenes in the Mediterranean region in various ways:

- through the collection of statistics on flows, markets and products: three seminars were held on this subject in the Mediterranean region between 1991 and 1993;

-       through procedures for the integration of Mediterranean countries in tourist policies: two seminars were held, in Istanbul in 1990 and in Bruges in 1992;

-       through special action programmes, for example in co-operation with the Turkish Government, promoting tourism in the countries of Eastern Europe, round the Black Sea and in Central Asia;

-       support for universities in the region: Tangier, Rome, Zagreb and Istanbul;

-       development projects within the framework of the United Nations Development Programme: Montenegro, Greece, Malta and Cyprus.

c.   **Other multilateral schemes.**

Apart from the WTO, which is a global intergovernmental organisation, other international institutions, in particular the United Nations Economic Commission for Europe, the International Labour Organisation and the International Labour Office, the International Maritime Organisation, the International Parliamentary Union, the CSCE, UNESCO and the Council of Europe have all contributed to the development of tourism in the Mediterranean. The European Bank for Reconstruction and Development (EBRD) has also launched campaigns to help countries of the East Mediterranean region, mainly in Albania.

In 1994, for example, the OECD organised a seminar on tourism and employment which, although extending beyond the confines of the Mediterranean countries, has nevertheless helped to pinpoint the most appropriate steps that could be taken to improve the tourist industry and reduce unemployment in the region.

Within the framework of its various conferences concerning the Mediterranean and surrounding countries, the Council of Europe has introduced two instruments designed to promote and co-ordinate the endeavours of member countries to set up marine or terrestrial reserves (European Network of Biogenetic Reserves and Convention on the conservation of European wildlife and natural habitats). UNESCO organised the adoption of the Ramsar Convention of 1971 on Wetlands of International Importance Especially as Waterfowl Habitat.

d.   **The Convention for the Protection of the Mediterranean Sea Against Pollution and its protocols.**

The Convention for the Protection of the Mediterranean Sea against Pollution was adopted on 16 February 1976 in Barcelona. It contains twenty-nine Articles and an Appendix concerning the arbitration procedure.

In the years following the signature of this international convention under the aegis of the United Nations Environment Programme (UNEP), a number of protocols were drawn up inciting states to take specific action against widespread pollution or to co-operate in one way or another in managing the environment.

Five protocols already exist:

-        Protocol for the prevention of pollution of the Mediterranean sea by dumping from ships and aircraft,

-        Protocol concerning co-operation in combating pollution of the Mediterranean sea by oil and other harmful substances in cases of emergency,

-        Protocol for the protection of the Mediterranean sea against pollution from land-based sources,

-        Protocol concerning Mediterranean specially protected areas,

-        Protocol concerning pollution resulting from exploration and exploitation of the continental shelf and the seabed and its subsoil.

"This flexible formula seemed well suited to the needs of the region. It is clear that despite a shared perception of a common regional problem, the coastal States of the Mediterranean are economically and politically heterogeneous. With a framework convention and "optional" protocols, States may accept the general legal obligation to protect their shared sea and progressively may assume more specific duties as the national economic, social and political climate permits."

The Barcelona Convention made it possible to define the fundamental characteristics of the Mediterranean Action Plan in operational terms, including the following aspects:

-        evaluation: determining and evaluating the causes, extent and consequences of environmental problems. The most important activities concern the evaluation of marine pollution and the study of coastal and marine activities and socio-economic factors which can have an impact on the degradation of the environment or suffer the consequences of such degradation;

-        management: the purpose of evaluation is to gather information which will help those responsible to achieve more efficient and effective management of their natural resources;

-        the legal framework: the Convention provides the legal framework for all national and regional co-operation schemes. By entering into legal commitments, governments clearly express their political resolve to deal with environmental problems either individually or together with other governments affected by the same problems;

-        the institutional framework: the programme is carried out mainly through national institutions assigned to the task and a number of co-ordinating bodies, including:

-        the Mediterranean Action Plan (MAP) Co-ordination Unit established

56

in Athens since 1982,
- the Regional Activities Centre for the Priority Action Programme (RAC/PAP) in Split (Croatia),
- the Regional Activities Centre of the Blue Plan (RAC/BP) Sophia Antipolis (France),
- the Regional Maritime Pollution Emergency Response Centre for the Mediterranean Sea (RAC/RMPERC) Malta,
- the Regional Activities Centre for Specially Protected Areas (RAC/SPA) in Tunis Salambo, Tunisia;

- funding: the UNEP, other UN bodies and the European Community provided the capital required for launching the campaign or financial aid which acted as a catalyst when the programmes were being drawn up. However, once a programme has been implemented regional governments and users (ie specialists, researchers and companies) are expected to gradually take over financial responsibility for it.

These formed the basis of the first ministerial conference on tourism within sustainable development held at Hyères-les-Palmiers (Var, France). During the conference a Euro-Mediterranean Declaration on Tourism within Sustainable Development (see Appendix I) was adopted. This meeting took place at a time when the development of Mediterranean tourism had reached a turning point, after which the interaction between maritime, coastal and hinterland areas and the persons responsible for such problems would be dealt with in a more innovatory manner with a view to meeting the challenges of the forthcoming years.

The Hyères Conference was a milestone on the road towards harmonisation of policies and strategies for Mediterranean tourism compatible with sustainable development and co-operation between those directly and indirectly engaged in this capital sector of activity:

- through increased awareness of the problems of ensuring that the sea, the land and the population suffer no harm from tourism even in the long term,

- through the undertakings by the countries concerned to adopt practical policies involving greater regional co-operation;

- through the pooling of knowledge and technical know-how so as to meet future challenges.

The Declaration adopted by the Ministers of Tourism of all the Mediterranean countries, on instructions from their governments, provides for the setting up of a network or an institution responsible for launching such co-operation.

Over a period of two years, the members of the Committee responsible for implementing the declaration drew up a series of co-operation projects which resulted in the Mediterranean Tourism Charter which was adopted by the responsible Ministers in Casablanca (Morocco) on 22 September 1995. This Charter was included in the agenda of the Barcelona Conference on Euro-Mediterranean Co-operation which took place in late November 1995.

THE MEDITERRANEAN TOURISM CHARTER

The Mediterranean States represented by their Minister of Tourism in the Conference in Casablanca held on 22 September 1995.

Conscious of the main role of the Mediterranean Basin within world tourism development;

Conscious of the impact of this development on an area wider than the Mediterranean seaboard;

Considering that security, stability and prosperity are necessary for maintaining peace in the area;

Considering the Euro-Mediterranean Ministerial Declaration on Tourism within Sustainable Development adopted in Hyères-les-Palmiers (France) on 23 September 1993, and other international documents on Mediterranean co-operation,

Recognise that :

The vitality of Mediterranean tourism is based on the Mediterranean identity and its authenticity,

The development of the area should be based on a planned approach integrated with other social and economic sectors, respecting the various cultures and the environment,

Increased co-operation is urgently needed to ensure the sustainable development of the whole region and the wellbeing of its populations.

The Mediterranean identity, which is the result of a long and common history, has to be protected, enhanced and promoted.

Mediterranean States shall confirm and develop their solidarity which is necessary for the harmonious development of tourism in the area.

For these reasons, with all the parties concerned, they commit themselves to respect a code of ethics, particularly in utilising the natural and cultural resources, building infrastructure and facilities, marketing and promoting Mediterranean products and services.

Tourist competition and co-operation shall be based on the respect of these ethics.

Furthermore, the Mediterranean States shall seek to eliminate all barriers to the freedom of lawful movements for Mediterranean people and for tourists from other parts of the world and ensure their security.

Conscious that a harmonious tourism with sustainable development cannot be achieved unless a close partnership is established between governments, local and regional authorities, private sectors and the population of host countries, the Mediterranean States shall try to initiate and promote such co-operation as stated in the declaration of Hyères-les-Palmiers. In this respect they shall seek to:

-    establish data banks for the exchange of information as far as possible using methods, instruments and standard data-collecting indicators in the field of tourism culture as well as environment;

-    preserve the common heritage and consolidate the Mediterranean identity, and promote them as well as the diversity of their resources through projects uniting Mediterranean routes of history and culture;

-    introduce innovative technologies and new management practices to improve the quality of tourist products and services;

-    encourage and facilitate investment through specific supportive action, by creating multilateral mechanisms notably structural and financial suitably adapted to Mediterranean realities;

-    propose codes of conduct concerning the activities of tourists and visitors in sensitive, fragile social, cultural or natural environments.

The Mediterranean States will:

-    co-operate for the promotion and the development of tourism in the Mediterranean, and

-    invite operators and local authorities to propose projects of good practice which will enable a more balanced spread of tourism activity in the whole Mediterranean basin and which can be used as models unifying other Mediterranean co-operation efforts;

-    invite the parties concerned to place emphasis on programmes creating new employment opportunities at the local level;

-    invite them to pursue a tourist development which encourages the participation of local communities which highlights the sectors linked to tourism, such as handicrafts and recreation;

-    commit themselves to support programmes for enhancing social and national tourism in the context of their collective commitment to the preservation of, and respect for, the individual identity and national heritage of Mediterranean nations.

Within the framework of defining the national tourist policies and in the perspective of reinforcing regional co-operation concerning this sector, the Mediterranean States decide to ensure the establishment of the Mediterranean Tourism Network, which is an instrument of co-operation among themselves and between states and local and regional authorities, tour operators and consumers' associations.

The network shall elaborate and offer the necessary means for the establishment of a long-term working programme between public and private sectors and for elevating tourism to its due place within sustainable development of the countries of the Mediterranean. It will also ensure the collective effort of promoting the Mediterranean quality and image by granting the Mediterranean label of quality and authenticity.

The Mediterranean Tourism Network will be authorised to act on behalf of the Mediterranean States vis-a-vis governmental and non-governmental international institutions concerned with tourism. In addition, it will serve as an organisational structure for the periodical meetings of Mediterranean Tourism Ministers.

PROTECTION OF LANDSCAPES IN THE PROCESS OF TOURIST DEVELOPMENT IN ESTONIA. ABSTRACT.

Toomas KOKOVKIN
Research Director, Hiiumaa Centre, Estonia

Landscape means the general shape and appearance of an area of land. Landscape is everything you can see when you look across an area of land, including hills, rivers, buildings and trees, etc. One could define it also as landscape view or paysage.

The other meaning of landscape is more scientific and implies a territorial approach. Landscapes can be regarded as internally uniform spatial formations in a certain territory, differing from each other primarily by the set of components. The components of landscapes (plant cover, soils, waters, land forms, etc.) are genetically inter-related, both in their development and spatial location. Change in one of its components will alter the whole of the complex and will make it develop as a new, entirely different entity.

When talking about landscape protection, people usually mean protection of the landscape view. The view is however only an appearance of a landscape region, looked upon from a certain location. This is why, in order to establish the protection of landscapes, we should look at the analysis with greater depth and talk about the protection of the co-existence of landscape components.

"Cultural landscape" is an interesting term to use in this sense. This is a human-shaped landscape, here artificial constructions have become its components. The cultural landscape may be described as one which is the result of additions and extractions to and from nature made by man.   This landscape aspect mirrors the functionalistic relations between man and nature (Königsson, 1990). Aside from natural landscapes, the cultural ones often include valuable examples of balanced man-nature interactions, and these vanishing worlds deserve as much protection as natural environments. Landscape reserves are created for this purpose. These are protected parts of the countryside which contribute to its beauty and variety, although recreation is given priority (Nature conservation in Estonia, 1994).

To promote tourism development it is important to protect the aesthetic qualities as well as the educational aspect of landscapes. Land use regulations and control of development (with the use of building permits, for example) should include sections on the protection of the visual quality of the landscape. This should be considered in development control particularly when choosing the locations of new constructions. This rule should apply to all construction, not just to tourism. It makes no difference whether the landscape's visual quality is destroyed by tourism development or some other type of development (Jaakson, 1995).

Estonia is a good example of an Eastern European country which imposes constraints in order to protect the landscape. In spite of its small territory (45,215 sq. km), Estonia is quite mosaic in its landscapes. The country itself is situated in the central part of the European plain and, as a whole, in the climatic zone of mixed forests. This variety is due to the relief shape and differences in the parent material of soils.

Various social, political and cultural factors influence landscapes. The following are some examples of the factors which have affected Estonia during the last few decades:

1.   **Long-lasting traditions to protect nature**. Despite the fact that the Soviet administration paid little attention to environmental conditions, protected natural areas were quite widespread and in general properly managed, due mostly to the total state ownership of the land.

2.   **Large-scale agriculture and the increase of forested areas** have shaped the Estonian countryside. The creation of enormous fields and the improvement of the wetlands, together with communist agricultural management after the Second World War, changed the former medium-scale private farm cultural landscapes. National parks and landscape reserves were established in the areas where examples of traditional country were preserved.

3.   **Military restrictions in coastal areas** from the 1950s to the 1990s have had the effect of destroying the social life of numerous Estonian coastal villages . As far as nature conservation is concerned, the restrictions had a very positive effect. As a result, the Estonian coasts are generally unspoiled and natural-looking.

Today, Estonia is re-creating a democratic state with a market economy. Land reform is under way, where the main emphasis is placed on restitution of land to its former owners. These changes place new pressures on nature protection policies, and new conflicts arise. The opening of the borders has created growth in foreign tourism in areas which are not acquainted with this industry at all.

The new market-oriented policy has resulted in tourism being now considered as a source of income in Estonia, as a sector which can improve the country's economy and, in particular, encourage the goods and service market, create new job opportunities, provide an exchange of international experience, bring in foreign currency thereby stabilise the balance of trade and strengthen the country's financial situation. The problems which today form barriers against the tourist trade are first and foremost the economic and structural weaknesses. Examples of these are an inferior infrastructure, low quality goods and services with an unreliable supply, a low standard of living (Nortra Consult AS).

Foreign visitors, approximately 1.5 million in 1993, represent the main part of tourists. Tourism represents 8% of the GNP, and 13.5% of country's exports. The tourist industry employs 54,000 people, i.e. 8% of the total workforce (*Eestiturismi arengumudel*, 1995).

Estonia has much to offer due to its cultural events, the interesting countryside and the relatively low prices. At the same time, tourism development lays a strong emphasis on unspoiled nature, which is a particular tourist attraction (*Eesti turismi arengumudel*, ibid). Environmental protection should therefore be properly controlled as the probable increase of touristic pressure on natural areas may gradually decrease the natural value of several sites. As a consequence, "nature consumption" will diminish and tourists will abandon the ecologically and culturally degraded areas. This could be likened to any living system which uses energy, matter and information and produces waste. Tourist landscapes are a sort of dump landscape with reduced diversity as they are trampled, minor facilities spread, then infrastructures and buildings spring up.

In order to avoid the degradation of the landscape, *inter alia*, due to tourism development, several measures are in progress or planned through Estonian legislation. The present legislative acts define the protection of various landscape components (coasts, forests) and are in some cases quite powerful. For instance, there is a legally enforced building restricted zone of 200 metres from the seashore of the islands and 100 metres on the mainland.

Protected areas cover about 7% of the Estonian territory. Today there are four state natural reserves, four national parks, one biosphere reserve and four hundred and seventy-nine (479) various protected areas, including thirteen landscape reserves (Nature Conservation in Estonia, 1994). But these measures are not sufficient to protect landscapes such as complex territorial formations, and several legislative acts are under preparation.

The future strategy for the environmental protection of Estonia will include a special part for the protection of landscape diversity. As regards tourism, the draft of this paper proposes the following actions (Sepp, 1995):

- inclusion of the tourism component into the management plans for protected areas;
- linking, at State budget level, the profits earned from tourism to the cost of nature protection;
- establishing a broad co-operation to develop tourism infrastructures;
- developing eco-tourism;
- promoting nature as an Estonian trademark.

The Estonian law for landscape protection is under preparation. This law has made an attempt to look at the landscape as a complex feature. Its main objectives are formulated as follows (Koljat, Ranniku, 1995):

- creation of preconditions for safeguarding human health and biodiversity through landscape protection and shaping its components
- conservation and development of characteristic views, aesthetics and variety of landscapes through their sustainable use.

The draft of this law prescribes that landscape protection should be carried out firstly through functional planning. Leading functions of landscapes are agriculture, forestry, protection, industry, urbanisation and recreation (Koljat, Ranniku, ibid).

Landscapes which are delineated by the State as recreational obviously have the strongest link to tourism. Special measures to maintain the landscapes have been proposed, thus, in the detailed planning of those landscapes, special action should be undertaken to increase their carrying capacity, also to avoid disturbing wildlife and the curative properties of landscapes.

The Estonian tourism development strategy foresees dividing the country into different touristic regions:

1. Tallin, the capital, and its surroundings;
2. the Western coast and islands of Hiiumaa and Saaremaa;
3. Pärnu town and the south-west;
4. Tartu town and its surroundings;
5. Vôru town and the south-east;
6. the North-east (*Eesti ruismi arenbumudel*, ibid.).

It is interesting to notice that this delineation corresponds roughly to the regions of Estonia's natural landscapes (Varep, 1987). Only the vast agricultural and wilderness areas in the central part of the country have been left out from the tourism managers' interests. At the same time, the unspoiled landscapes of the western coast and islands are being given special attention as "an area of great potential for nature tourism".

The west-Estonian archipelago is a biosphere reserve. Biosphere reserves are a special type of protected area where human development strategies are strongly associated with nature protection and sustainable use. Therefore, tourism development plans on the Estonian islands are mainly worked out as "eco" or "soft tourism" programmes. There are several examples of fruitful co-operation between tourism managers and nature protectionists on the Estonian islands.

ENVIRONMENTAL POLICY AND MANAGEMENT IN CYPRUS

Notes from the presentation by **N.S. GEORGIADES**
Director of the Environment Service
Ministry of Agriculture, natural Resources and
Environment, Athens, Greece

Historical perspective

-       consequences of 1974 invasion
-       rapid change / transformation / economic growth not exactly characterised by environmental sensitivity
-       some political institutions and organisations slow to evolve
-       local government appointed, devolution lagged behind

Tourism

-       one of developments that act. cumulative impacts
-       small country: land, water, labour, energy scarce
-       occupation

Factors affecting impacts
-       nature of tourism
-       number
-       seasonality
-       behaviour
-       ecosystem health
-       frameworks

Impacts
-       land uses
-       land values
-       loss of agricultural land
-       coastal transformation
-       pollution
-       noise
-       ecosystems
-       visual
-       on physical systems
-       on socio-economic structure
-       labour
-       cultural features
-       infrastructure and its impacts
-       move problems inland, infrastructure inadequate
-       other uses that follow with own problems
-       on rural settlements, rural houses

Overall environmental policy

<u>Guides</u>
- sustainable development
- integral environment considerations into those of economic and social development policy
- European Union

<u>Goals</u>
- safeguarding natural productive resources
- protection of biodiversity and ecosystems
- rectification of environmental damage
- strengthening existing institutional structure
- creation of environmental awareness
- participation
- modernisation and codification of environmental legislation
- integrated pollution and waste management control

Institutional framework - diagram

<u>Policy-making and Legislative Level</u>

<u>Council of Ministers</u>
- higher executive and policy-making body
- overall responsibility for formulation of environmental policy

<u>House of Parliament</u>
- no legislative or fiscal measures can be implemented without its approval
- parliamentary hearings

<u>Minister of Agriculture, Natural Resources and Environment</u>
- environment policy applied by the Council of Ministers through the Minister
- responsible to administer overall control and co-ordination over the protection and preservation of the environment [excluding town and county planning issues]

Objectives and Consultation Level

<u>Environmental Committee</u>
- chaired by PS / MANRE
- intergovernmental
- civil service part of executive branch
- interpretation of goals into objectives, programmes and plans
- safeguarding the quality of processes and decisions
- streamlining enforcement processes
- setting priorities:

[Theoretical]
- irreversibility
- rapid worsening
- gravity of consequences
- scale
- economic impact

[Actual]
- responsive and crisis management

- interdepartmental co-ordination and effective implementation
- building up institutional competence
- resolution of conflicts
- review and appraisal of programmes and suggestions
- exchange of information relating to the quality of the environment
- review environmental issues
- advise on formulation and determination of environmental policy objectives

Council for the Environment

- chaired by the Minister
- members governmental / quasi-governmental / non-governmental environmental / professional organisations
- advises on environmental issues
- recommends environmental policy and legislation
- co-ordinates public and private action
- pursues environmental awareness activities
- debates environmental problems
- forum of interaction
- dissemination of information
- first-hand knowledge as regards the concerns of various organisations

[Currently re-organised (representative) and mandate changed (sustainable development)]

Flow chart 1

Physical planning framework

**Environmental planning
and co-ordination framework**

Council of Ministers

Minister of Interior

Minister of Agriculture
and Natural Resources

Planning council

Permanent
Secretary (M.I.)

Planning Bureau

Permanent Secretary
(M.A.W.R.)

Department of
town planning
and housing

Environment Service

Ministries/Department with
executive responsibilities and
local government

Council for the
protection of the
environment

Environment
Committe

Co-ordination and Implementation Level

Environment Service
Permanent Secretary's Office

-        functional and executive
-        advises on environmental policy
-        co-ordinates Government environmental programmes
-        ensures implementation of environmental policy
-        technical committee on environmental impact assessments
-        administers Law on the control of Water Pollution
-        co-ordinates process for adoption of EU policy and legislation
-        co-ordinates co-operation with international agencies
-        promotes environmental awareness
-        training
-        information
-        identification and analysis of problems
-        assistance, guidance, advise and monitoring
-        fosters environmental policies and programmes
-        encourages prevention and abatement practices
-        recommends methods for minimizing impacts
-        administrative support to Committee and Council
-        National Focal Point (CSD), INFOTERRA, UNEP, Basel, CITES, Bern, Montreal, Biological Diversity, Climate Change

Strategy pursued
-        facilitating framework in outreach and rallying support efforts
-        setting up priorities as far as this may be achieved
-        learning from errors and pursuing goal redefinition
-        establishing credibility and performance
-        refraining from being identified with any specific group
-        adopting a cross-media approach
-        aiming at securing outcomes through consensus negotiation

Operational effectiveness
-        decisions taken in open and explainable way
-        departments acting in the best public interest
-        ease of contact and effective communication between all the actors in the process
-        objective decisions
-        public incorporated into the decision-making process
-        legal and administrative implementability
-        existing institutions enhanced

Co-ordination and linkages
-        policies to be properly integrated, common purposes established, a systems approach achieved
-        not excessively hierarchical
-        roles of every agency clearly defined

- implementation by diverse agencies (varieties in task environment and clientele)
- effective mechanism for sharing information, policy integration and co-ordination
- issues-oriented, problem solving, systems approach relying on strong co-ordination
- critical linkages
- physical planning
- tourism management
- natural resources
- normative authorities

National legal framework

Broader
- Town and Country Planning Law
- Fisheries Law and Regulations
- Forestry Legislation
- Game and Fauna Law

Environment - specific

Approved
- Water Pollution Control Law
- Air Pollution Control Law
- Dangerous Substances Law
- Agrochemicals
- Pollution of Public Spaces

Prepared
- Framework Law on the Environment
  - precautionary principle
  - civil liability
  - compensation for damages
  - injunctions
- Framework Law on the Protection of Nature
- Soil pollution
- Special Waste
- Noise
- Chemicals, Industrial Accidents and Biotechnology
- Protection of nature and wildlife
- Ionising Radiation
- Fertilisers
- Climate change Convention
- Biological Diversity Convention

New Action Plan

Rio, Barabados, Tunis, European Union

- Fiscal
- Information
- Research
- Participation

Subjects
- General Policy
- Water protection and management
- Waste management
- Radiation
- Atmosphère
- Noise
- Chemicals, Industrial Accidents and Biotechnology
- Protection of nature and wildlife

Major Studies
- Management of Hazardous Waste
- Use of Fiscal Instruments
- Management of Akamas Peninsula
- Rural Sanitation
- Recycling of Domestic Solid Waste
- Used Machine Oils
- National Waste Management Strategy
- Integrated Environmental Information System
- Assessment of the Carrying Capacity of the Coastal Zone
- Enhancement of Environmental Impact Assessment Capacity
- Preparation of Detailed Action Plans for Streamlining the Country's Environmental Policy with that of the European Union
- Use and Release of Genetically Modified Organisms

Fiscal instruments

Principal objectives
- support implementation of sound land use policies and coastal zone management practices for sustainable development
- assist in introduction of such instruments in the overall environmental planning process

Role - general
- internalising externalities imposed on the environment: 'polluters' face full costs of actions
- incentives for polluters (in broader sense) to change behaviour
- raising revenue which can be used for environmental matters
- compensating individuals for loss of economic benefits arising from conservation and contribution to the public good

Role - Cyprus
- slow down coastal development and enhance quality of development
- improve allocation of water resources and encourage more efficient water use by all sectors
- protect natural and cultural heritage
- ensure that all 'polluters' - whether industrialists, developers or households producing waste - are aware of the full costs associated with their actions
- encourage conservation

Instruments assessed
- sixteen economic instruments identified - Table
- evaluation based on:
  - efficiency
  - effectiveness
  - ease of implementation
  - acceptability
  - compatibility with other policy instruments and initiatives

Shortlist of potential instruments

User charges
- based on level of waste production to provide clearer incentives to reduce environmental impact/demand on services

Pricing for water resource management
- increase efficiency through pricing water at the marginal cost of supply: however, correct marginal cost uncertain
- raising water prices more equitable than current situation however,
  - may not lead to overall reduction in water use
  - some short-term reductions in demand for irrigation water
  - may lead to decisions to develop new irrigation schemes to take up excess supply
  - higher water prices would make some current farming enterprises unprofitable and conflict with wider social objectives
  - difficult decisions

Environmental development charge
- incentives to slow down rate of new investments (costs of developments would be increased)
- raise revenue for environmental projects
- levied on the floor area of new buildings: exceptions
- level set so as to offset marginal damage cost (survey based valuation techniques)
- structured to provide incentives to invest in less environmentally sensitive areas

Transferable development rights
-		some rights to develop on a different, not protected site
-		traded in the market through local estate agents
-		permitted area for transfer established through a formula similar to that already
		used for listed buildings
-		purchasers of TDRs allowed increased building density in designated tourist
		or commercial development zones

Development completion bonds
-		similar to those in use for major infrastructure projects
-		cover domestic and commercial property
-		bond discharged on satisfactory completion of project

Environment fund
-		revenue from instruments:
		-		revert to general taxation
		-		earmarked for specific purposes
		-		recycled to environment fund
-		additional funding important to realise a number of environmental objectives
-		core funding by Environment Development Charge

Barriers to introduction
-		widespread perception that taxation levels are high
-		general resistance to increased taxation
-		limited awareness of environmental quality
-		strong emphasis on individual rights to develop land and property

Means of overcoming barriers
-		charging system transparent and fair
-		revenue earmarked to support environmental investments
-		fiscally neutral: compensatory reductions in other taxation
-		when introduced, accompanied by targeted information
-		gradual introduction

Conclusion
-		combination of charges and earmarked Environmental Fund important stimuli
		to stronger environmental management and the realisation of environmental
		objectives

Environmental impact assessment

-		mining and quarrying in 1990
-		integrated system approved in 1991
-		system in place mostly based on EU Directive 337/85
-		UNEP's approach also influenced the system
-		formalise in Framework Law

[Flowcharts 2 and 3]
-         two-stage procedure - 1) Preliminary Environmental Impact Assessment
          (PEIA), 2) Full Environmental Impac Assessment (EIA)

*   two-stage procedure - Preliminary Environmental Impact Assessment (PEIA)
          / full Environmental Impact Assessment (EIA)

Projects covered
-         large projects of public and private sector with estimated cost of construction
          exceeding $ 2/1 million
-         projects located outside local plan areas, village development boundaries,
          animal husbandry areas and industrial zones of limited degree of nuisance

Independently of above
-         tourist installations and residential building complexes covering an area of
          more than four hectares
-         aquaculture projects
-         coastal camping sites
-         recreation areas and sporting facilities covering an area of more than two
          hectares
-         coastal improvement and protection structures
-         ports, marinas, fishing shelters and breakwaters
-         waste water and sludge treatment plants
-         solid and liquid disposal areas
-         toxic and hazardous wastes disposal areas
-         animal husbandry areas
-         hospital installations
-         dams and diversion of river stems
-         roads with more than two lanes
-         land consolidation schemes
-         mining and quarrying activities
-         crashing plants
-         industrial installations and industrial areas
-         power plants and telecommunication installations
-         reforestation projects
-         airports and heliports

**Flowchart for the Preparation
of Preliminary Environmental Impact Assessment (PEIA)**

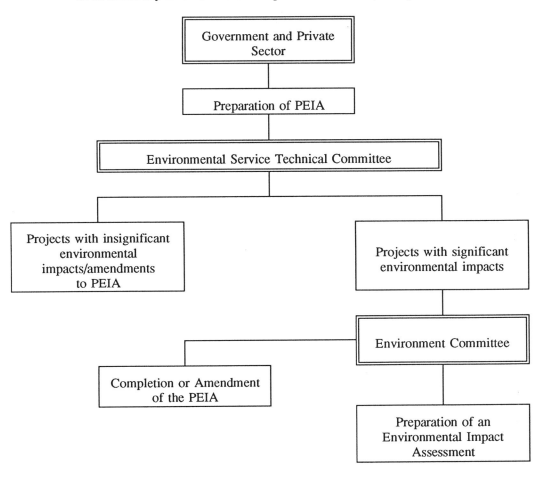

Key

_____   Direction

☐   Committee or Organisation

☐   Decision/Action

Flowchart 3

**Flowchart for the Preparation
of Environmental Impact Assessment (EIA)**

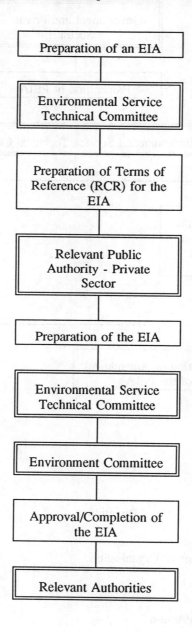

Preparation of an EIA

Environmental Service
Technical Committee

Preparation of Terms of
Reference (RCR) for the
EIA

Relevant Public
Authority - Private
Sector

Preparation of the EIA

Environmental Service
Technical Committee

Environment Committee

Approval/Completion of
the EIA

Relevant Authorities

Task environment factors shaping policies in 1990s

<u>Positive</u>
-       government's strong environmental agenda
-       political parties publicly support measures for the conservation of the environment
-       political and decision-making system highly pluralistic
-       division of power fully functioning
-       press and a large number of private radio and television stations
-       local councils elected, representative, accountable
-       people calling for action by their elected representatives and the Ministers, rather than by the bureaucracy
-       large number of non-governmental organisations eventually surfaced
-       civil servants no longer protected from the politics of their decision, technical expertise contested, no longer accepted as the sole custodians of the public interest
-       changes in peoples' values and priorities
-       growing recognition that sustainability of tourism and irrigated agriculture rely on the quality of the environment
-       new actors are entering the decision-making arena
-       environmental concerns mushrooming and emerging from the twilight zone

<u>Negative</u>
-       short-term perspective, neglect of the longer-term view
-       transformation from mostly agricultural to services and information oriented society
-       economic self interest vs. public consciousness
-       high individualism
-       land relationship / ownership / constitutional safeguards of land / inheritance customs and traditions
-       bureaucracy not sufficiently prepared to deal with the socio-cultural, political and psychological complexities inherent in the evolution of an environmental policy
-       NIMBY, LULU, BANANA at apotheosis
-       ignorance and fear
-       needs of economic development not ceased
-       individual agendas aggressively demanding acting on all fronts
-       proliferation of actions and commitments, difficult to shelve those that may end up having a low degree of priority
-       minefield of uncertainty
-       diffused variety of conflicting interests
-       reconciling differing concerns within a context characterised by shortage of consensus, in the public-at-large, regarding the qualities of the preferred environment

<u>Overall</u>
-      trends favouring more environmentally sensitive policies

<u>Greater factor for success</u>
-      road to European Union

COASTAL EROSION IN AND PROTECTIVE MEASURES

Xenia LOIZIDOU
Public Works Department, Cyprus

ABSTRACT

The coastal area is an area of continuous morphological changes, due to its dynamic behaviour and its rapid response to any natural changes or human interventions. The construction of coastal structures, the intensive mining of beach material and river damming are some of the main human activities which cause morphological changes to the coastal zone, by changing the hydrodynamic regime and the dynamic status of the near shore areas.

The coastal zone is an area of vital economic importance for an island country like Cyprus. After the Turkish invasion of 1971 and the occupation of 40% of the island's territory, the free coastal areas have been heavily exploited and have experienced a continuously increasing pressure, due to the effort of reconstruction and revitalisation of the economy. While the 2 metre-wide coastal zone covers only 13% of the island's area, 40% of the population live and work there and it is the basis of 90% of the tourist industry, which is the main economic activity in Cyprus. All this overloading of the coast resulted in morphological and environmental problems in some areas. The morphological problem of coastal erosion became serious in some areas and measures had to be taken in order to protect the eroding coasts.

Considering the coasts as natural resource for Cyprus, it was recognised that a coherent strategic framework was needed in order to reconcile development requirements and exploitation, with the need to protect, to conserve and where necessary improve the coastal areas. As part of this effort, the Cypriot Government co-financed the Study "Coastal Zone Management of Cyprus", through the European Union programme MEDSPA. The Study started in February 1993 and is expected to finish by December 1995. It is carried out by the Coastal Unit of the Public Works Department, Ministry of Communications and Works, in joint co-operation with the Delft Hydraulics Institute.

The Study mainly focuses on shoreline management, which is a part of Coastal Zone Management. The basic objective of the Study is to find proper methods to protect the coastline and improve the quality of the beach where necessary, without any serious consequences to the environment. The expected outcome of the Project is the creation of Master Plans for coastal protection and improvement works for specific priority areas and the formulation of coherent regional strategies and policies concerning the protection, conservation and improvement, where needed, of the coast.

THE DEVELOPMENT OF TOURISM IN CENTRAL AND EASTERN EUROPEAN COUNTRIES AND IDENTIFICATION OF ITS SPECIFIC IMPACT ON THEIR NATURAL ENVIRONMENT

Peter SHACKLEFORD
World Tourism Organization, Spain

Europe is still the most popular destination for international tourism. A European country, France, received the largest number of tourists in 1994, some 60,640,000 people. Other European countries which feature in the top twenty tourist destinations are Spain, Italy, Hungary, United Kingdom, Poland, Austria, Czech Republic, Germany, Switzerland, Greece, Portugal and The Netherlands. European countries also number among the world's highest spenders on tourism; expenditure by Germany, the United Kingdom, France, Italy, The Netherlands and Austria being especially significant. However, while western Europe has tended to mark time or even lose market share compared with other world regions such as East Asia and the Pacific, the countries of Central and Eastern Europe have, in recent years, been experiencing significant growth. As the accompanying tables show, Southern Europe in 1994 accounted for 29.5 per cent of arrivals in Europe and 33.5 per cent of receipts. At the same time Central and Eastern Europe accounted for 21.8 per cent of arrivals but only 6.6 per cent of receipts. What is clear however, is that tourist arrivals in Central and Eastern European tourist destinations are growing very rapidly, as the double-figure growth level recorded by Albania, Croatia, Slovenia, Russian Federation, Poland and the Czech Republic shows.

The significance of this fast-track development in Central and Eastern European destinations is that tourism is placing pressures upon the natural and built environment of these countries. Accordingly, it is a matter of urgency to take careful steps in order to plan tourism and ensure that existing tourist development is consistent with the principles of sustainable development adopted at the Rio Earth Summit.

Under its environment and planning programme carried out under the supervision of a committee composed of governments, the 'Environment Committee', WTO is able to address the environmental concerns of its Members and, in particular, those with economies in transition in Central and Eastern Europe. Given the widespread trend towards decentralized planning, the first step taken by WTO was the preparation and dissemination of methodologies concerning tourism planning. These include **Sustainable Tourism Development: Guide for Local Planners, Guidelines: Development of National Parks and Protected Areas for Tourism** and An Integrated Approach to Resort Development based upon six case studies, including cases from Europe.

Having thus addressed planning issues, WTO's second concern was to assist countries in evaluating the present and potential impacts of tourist development. In the opinion of WTO experts, this monitoring process was best accomplished by a series of tourism and environmental indicators. A user's guide to eleven basic environmental indicators, which have already been field tested in various countries, is in the process of being published.

The third thrust of WTO's environment programme was to address practical issues faced by countries. Documents under this heading include a guide to coastal zone management with particular reference to bathing beaches, guidance for the environmental management of hotels, a handbook on natural disaster reduction in tourist areas prepared in co-operation with the World Meteorological Organization (WMO), a guide for the management of built world heritage sites prepared in co-operation with the International Council on Monuments and Sites (ICOMOS) as well as an education and awareness creation programme directed at tour operators and other travel industry partners. In order to avoid duplication, WTO works closely with the United Nations Environment Programme (UNEP) and other relevant international organizations and recognizes the significant efforts carried out by the Council of Europe in, for example, nature tourism and rural tourism.

A recent development has been the publication by WTO, in co-operation with the World Travel and Tourism Council (WTTC) and the Earth Council, of a study of tourism implications of **Agenda 21**. The aim of this project was to adapt the general recommendations of UNCED's **Agenda 21** to the specific situation and requirements of the worldwide travel and tourism industry. Copies of this joint study, which has been distributed as a consultative document, have been issued to the participants attending the present Colloquy.

Finally, it should be mentioned that WTO conducts sectoral support missions and technical co-operation projects as an executing agency of the United Nations Development Programme in Central and Eastern European countries. Examples of recent environment-related projects and missions carried out in these countries include:

ALBANIA	Development of guidelines for coastal tourism
BELARUS	Development of hotel and restaurant networks
BULGARIA	The Monasteries Route
CROATIA	Marketing needs of the tourism sector
HUNGARY	Investment promotion
KAZAKHSTAN	Silk Road promotion
KYRGYZSTAN	Silk Road promotion
MOLDOVA	Tourism master plan
POLAND	Preservation and development of Cracow
ROMANIA	Development of spa resorts
RUSSIAN FEDERATION	Pilot project on ecotourism
SLOVENIA	Tourism sector assessment

TURKMENISTAN	Silk Road promotion
UKRAINE	Tourism marketing
UZBEKISTAN	Cultural heritage and Silk Road

In conclusion, by carrying out these studies and providing these services to its Members, WTO is able to contribute to the sustainable development of Central and Eastern European countries.

TOURISM MARKET TRENDS
WORLD'S TOP 40 TOURISM DESTINATIONS
International tourist arrivals (excluding same-day visitors)
(Arrivals in thousands) - 1994

Rank		Countries	Arrivals (000)	% change	% of total
1985	1994		1994	1994/93	1994
1	1	FRANCE	60 640	0.90	11.28
3	2	UNITED STATES	45 504	- 0.60	8.47
2	3	SPAIN	43 232	7.85	8.05
4	4	ITALY	27 480	4.17	5.11
11	5	HUNGARY	21 425	- 6.05	3.99
13	6	CHINA	21 070	11.00	3.92
6	7	UNITED KINGDOM	20 855	7.01	3.88
22	8	POLAND	18 800	10.59	3.50
5	9	AUSTRIA	17 894	- 1.99	3.33
9	10	MEXICO	17 113	3.50	3.18
16 (1)	11	CZECH REPUBLIC TCHÈQUE	17 000	47.83	3.16
7	12	CANADA	15 971	5.73	2.97
8	13	GERMANY	14 494	1.02	2.70
10	14	SWITZERLAND	12 200	- 1.61	2.27
14	15	GREECE	10 072	7.00	1.87
18	16	HONG KONG	9 331	4.40	1.74
15	17	PORTUGAL	9 132	3.28	1.70

21	18	MALAYSIA	7 197	10.65	1.34
23	19	SINGAPORE	6 268	7.99	1.17
20	20	NETHERLANDS	6 178	7.31	1.15
26	21	THAILAND	6 166	7.03	1.15
28	22	TURKEY	6 034	2.20	1.12
17 (2)	23	RUSSIAN FEDERATI RUSSIE	4 643	- 21.25	0.86
35	24	MACAO	4 489	14.66	0.84
24	25	IRLAND	4 309	10.83	0.80
19	26	BULGARIA	4 055	5.96	0.75
54	27	INDONESIA	4 006	17.72	0.75
55	28	SOUTH AFRICA	3 897	16.05	0.73
38	29	ARGENTINA	3 866	9.46	0.72
32	30	TUNISIA	3 856	5.47	0.72
40	31	KOREA REPUBLIC CORÉE	3 580	7.48	0.67
29	32	MOROCCO	3 465	- 13.96	0.64
46	33	AUSTRALIA	3 362	12.22	0.63
25	34	BELGIUM	3 304	0.58	0.61
36	35	PUERTO RICO	3 042	6.59	0.57
33	36	NORWAY	2 830	10.72	0.53
27	37	ROMANIA	2 796	- 3.95	0.52
41	38	EGYPT	2 356	2.84	0.44
-	39	CROATIA	2 293	50.76	0.43
47	40	URUGUAY	2 175	8.59	0.40
		TOTAL 1-40	**476 380**	**4.81**	**88.65**
		WORLD TOTAL	**537 366**	**4.96**	**100.00**

Source : World Tourism Organisation (WOT)
(1)   Former Czechoslovakia   (2)   Former USSR

WORLD'S TOP 20 TOURISM SPENDERS
International tourism expenditure (excluding transport)
(million US$) - 1994

Rank		Countries	Expenditure (mn US$)	% change	% of total
1985	1994		1994	1994/93	1994
1	1	UNITED STATES	43 562	7.00	14.28
2	2	GERMANY	41 753	11.30	13.69
4	3	JAPAN	30 715	14.35	10.07
3	4	UNITED KINGDOM	18 303	5.00	6.00
5	5	FRANCE	13 875	8.09	4.55
10	6	ITALY	12 181	- 6.68	3.99
6	7	CANADA	11 676	9.85	3.83
7	8	NETHERLANDS	10 983	22.39	3.60
8	9	AUSTRIA	9 330	14.06	3.06
17	10	TAIWAN	7 885	3.96	2.59
12	11	BELGIUM	7 735	21.56	2.54
9	12	SWITZERLAND	6 325	6.93	2.07
11	13	MEXICO	5 363	- 3.58	1.76
14	14	SWEDEN	4 878	9.27	1.60
15	15	AUSTRALIA	4 339	5.83	1.42
21	16	SPAIN	4 106	- 12.75	1.35
25	17	KOREA REPUBLIC	4 088	25.44	1.34
16	18	NORWAY	3 930	10.24	1.29
24	19	SINGAPORE	3 665	21.28	1.20
18	20	DENMARK	3 583	11.48	1.17
		TOTAL 1-20	248 275	8.92	81.40
		WORLD TOTAL	305 000	13.24	100.00

Source : World Tourism Organisation (WTO)

SOUTHERN EUROPE MARKET SHARE - 1994
(% of total Europe)

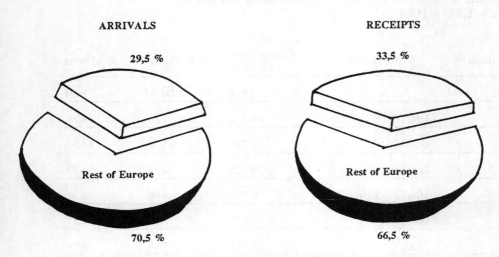

ARRIVALS

29,5 %

Rest of Europe

70,5 %

RECEIPTS

33,5 %

Rest of Europe

66,5 %

FASTEST GROWING SOUTHERN EUROPEAN DESTINATIONS
1985-1994

Average annual growth rate (%)

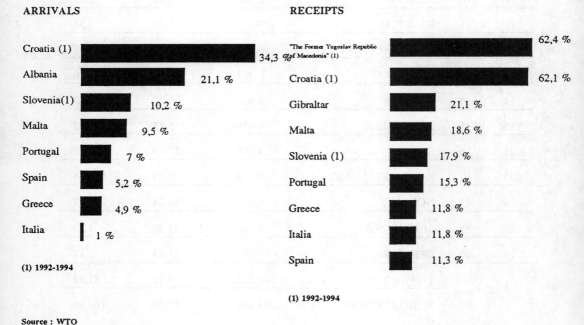

ARRIVALS

Croatia (1)	34,3 %
Albania	21,1 %
Slovenia(1)	10,2 %
Malta	9,5 %
Portugal	7 %
Spain	5,2 %
Greece	4,9 %
Italia	1 %

(1) 1992-1994

RECEIPTS

"The Former Yugoslav Republic of Macedonia" (1)	62,4 %
Croatia (1)	62,1 %
Gibraltar	21,1 %
Malta	18,6 %
Slovenia (1)	17,9 %
Portugal	15,3 %
Greece	11,8 %
Italia	11,8 %
Spain	11,3 %

(1) 1992-1994

Source : WTO

CENTRAL/EAST EUROPE MARKET SHARE - 1994
(% of total Europe)

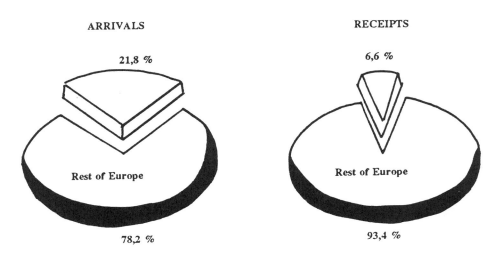

ARRIVALS

21,8 %

Rest of Europe

78,2 %

RECEIPTS

6,6 %

Rest of Europe

93,4 %

FASTEST GROWING CENTRAL/EAST EUROPEAN DESTINATIONS
1985-1994

Average annual growth rate (%)

ARRIVALS

RECEIPTS

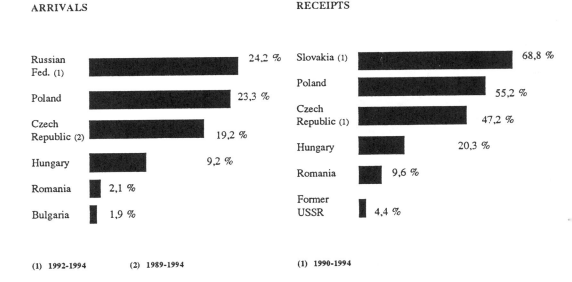

ARRIVALS	
Russian Fed. (1)	24,2 %
Poland	23,3 %
Czech Republic (2)	19,2 %
Hungary	9,2 %
Romania	2,1 %
Bulgaria	1,9 %

RECEIPTS	
Slovakia (1)	68,8 %
Poland	55,2 %
Czech Republic (1)	47,2 %
Hungary	20,3 %
Romania	9,6 %
Former USSR	4,4 %

(1) 1992-1994   (2) 1989-1994

(1) 1990-1994

Source : WTO

EAST MEDITERRANEAN EUROPE MARKET SHARE - 1994
(% of total Europe)

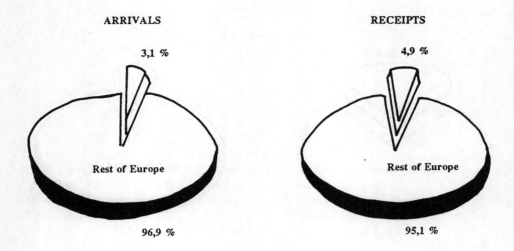

ARRIVALS

3,1 %

Rest of Europe

96,9 %

RECEIPTS

4,9 %

Rest of Europe

95,1 %

FASTEST GROWING EAST MEDITARRANEAN EUROPE DESTINATIONS
1985-1994

Average annual growth rate (%)

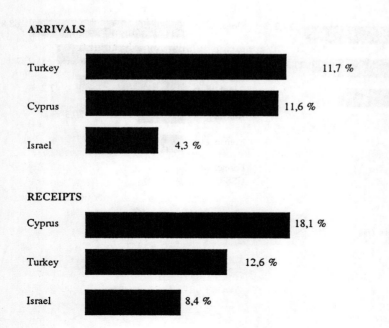

ARRIVALS

Turkey   11,7 %

Cyprus   11,6 %

Israel   4,3 %

RECEIPTS

Cyprus   18,1 %

Turkey   12,6 %

Israel   8,4 %

Source : WTO

POLLUTION: LEGAL MEANS FOR THE CONTROL OF WASTE AND SEWAGE

Anthony ELLUL
Malta

INTRODUCTION

The Environmental system works in an equilibrium. This equilibrium is dynamic, not static, and the component parts are continuously modified in response to fluctuating input and throughput of energy and matter. The system is self-regulating and in this way a balance is kept between the inter-related parts. 'Such a system has a structure of inter-relations that endows the entire community with a predictable developmental pattern, called "succession", that enables the community to make the best use of the physical environment'. (Woodwell, 1967).

However, this equilibrium has been disturbed, particularly as a result of man's interventions and his actions. Apart from natural disturbances (e.g. volcanic eruptions, earthquakes), human disturbances have, over the last decades, caused considerable harm to the environment and its resources. Pollution is only one of these environmental disturbances, but one whose effects extend much further than the locality in which it has been created, affecting other communities which are probably not benefiting from those industries creating the pollution. The nature of pollution is such that in most cases the consequences of such actions are felt in localities and by people further away from the source emitting the pollution.

The term pollution can be simply defined as any action leading to an abnormal environmental condition that upsets the environmental equilibrium. Such disturbances must not be limited solely to the natural system, but should also include disturbance to the socio-cultural system.

The various forms of pollution can be grouped under the following categories; **Water, Air, Noise, Waste** and **Visual**.

I would also add another type of pollution which is more closely associated with tourism activity and this could be termed as social pollution. This form of pollution refers to the disruption of social life as a result of pressures from tourist activity, thus creating social stress and hostility towards tourists by the local community.

ENVIRONMENTAL LEGISLATION IN THE EUROPEAN UNION

'The concept "environment" was virtually unknown in legal language before 1970... However, during the past two decades much attention has been focused on environmental law and many legislative provisions have been enacted to deal with environmental problems' (Aquilina, 1994).

The European Union, then the European Community, with the coming into force of the *Single European Act* of 1987, 'introduced, for the first time, two explicit references to the Community's powers in the field of environment protection: Article 100a lays down the criteria for environmental protection legislation affecting the internal market and allows legislation to be adopted by qualified majority in the Council. Articles 130r, 130s and 130t lay down the goals, means and procedure for the adoption of legislation regarding the environment, but by unanimous decision'. (Commission of the European Communities, DG, XI, 1992).

The goals and elements of environmental protection actions by the European Union set out in these articles are:

- to preserve, protect and improve the quality of the environment;
- to contribute towards protecting human health;
- to ensure a prudent and rational utilization of natural resources.

The European Union environmental protection actions are based on three principles:

- preventive action should be taken;
- environmental damage should be rectified at source;
- the polluter should pay;
- integration of environment into other Community policies.

Environmental legislation sets the minimum standards and member States are not prevented from introducing higher standards.

TOURISM AND POLLUTION FROM SOLID AND LIQUID WASTE

A survey carried out in 1991 asked several hundred environmentalists, who have been elected to the United Nations 500 Roll of Honour, which to them were the most problematic industries as regards pollution of the environment, and tourism ranked very low on the list, which was topped by the chemical and power generation industries. However, it was expected that tourism would rank higher on the list in future, unless measures to ensure a more sustainable development of the sector are taken.

Tourism certainly contributes to an increase in pollution from both solid and liquid waste. Although, it would be difficult to obtain accurate statistics regarding the level of pollution resulting from tourism development, nonetheless some estimations have been made. In Malta, no distinction can be made with regards to solid waste from domestic sources and tourism sources since all such waste is collected together. As regards the disposal of liquid waste generated, only estimates can be made.

The Sewage Master Plan for the Maltese Islands has estimated that the average daily consumption of water by a tourist is 250 litres. On the assumption that 80% of the water consumed becomes waste water, it is estimated that each tourist would create 200 litres of waste water per day. (CowiConsult, 1992).

A study on the tourism carrying capacity of Venice estimated that tourists staying in Venice produce 2.3 kg of waste each day. (Paolo Costa, 1988).

The Blue Plan for the Mediterranean estimates that the level of tourism activity in the Mediterranean by 2025 would create between 0.9 and 0.5 million cubic metres of waste water and between 8.7 and 12.1 million tonnes of waste per year. (Grenon and Barisse, 1988).

The above are only estimates, yet they may provide some measure of waste and sewage generated as a result of tourism development. There is no doubt that the production of waste and sewage cannot be eliminated. Development itself creates this waste. Yet the pollution created by both waste and sewage can be heavily reduced.

WASTE

Pollution from waste can be reduced by producing less waste, ensuring an effective and efficient waste collection system and improving the methods for the disposal of the waste created. It is estimated that the European Union generates over 2 billion tonnes of waste each year, of which 80% can be recycled, others are toxic and others can be avoided through the use of better technology. The Council Directive 75/422/EEC of 1975 of the European Union, deals with waste. This Directive recognises that the solution in reducing pollution from waste generation is not by implementing legal measures to ensure the appropriate disposal of the waste, but more importantly by first preventing or reducing waste production, and by formulating a waste management plan.

The reduction of waste production can be achieved by using better and clean technology, better product design and marketing and through the recovery of waste by means of recycling and re-use. Article 4 states that in the process of retrieving and disposing of waste, no harm should be done to human health and should not create any adverse effects on the environmental resources and should cause no nuisance.

The waste management plan should address the following issues:

- the type, quantity and origin of waste to be recovered or disposed of
- general technical requirements
- any special arrangements for particular wastes
- suitable disposal sites or installations

The same Directive lists a number of disposal operations and specifies that such operations require a permit from the competent authority in the country where the disposal is to be carried out. Such a permit shall cover:

- the types and quantities of waste
- the technical requirements
- the security precautions to be taken
- the disposal site
- the treatment method

Establishments carrying out their own waste disposal are exempted from such a permit under certain conditions.

Information as regards waste production and disposal is not available or even collected in many countries. The Directive compels establishments involved in disposal operations to collect such information which would include keeping records of the quantity, nature, origin and destination of the waste disposed, frequency of collection, transport mode and treatment method.

The Directive also states that, on the basis of the polluter pays principle, the cost of disposing of waste must be borne by the holder of waste or the producer of the product from which the waste came.

The European Union recognises that through just a legal framework, although the problem of pollution from solid waste disposal can be adequately addressed, the problem of waste generation requires a definite strategy. As part of its sectoral policy documents, the EU produced a document on a Waste Management Strategy. This strategy looks at the problem of waste in the medium and long-term and proposed a list of concrete action which should ensure the full and correct implementation of waste management legislation by Member States. This document identifies five strategic guidelines:

a.   prevention of waste through the use of cleaner technology and by minimizing waste at product level by taking into account the environmental impact of the entire product life cycle. It must be ensured that products placed on the market make the smallest possible contribution, by manufacture, use of final disposal to increase the amount of waste. Ecological labelling schemes are used in some countries.

b.   recycling and re-use of waste generated. This can take various forms including regeneration, raw materials recovery and energy conversion.

c.   optimization of final disposal. Dumping of waste should be considered as the last resort in waste management, and any treatment prior to dumping must be considered. Dumping should also be carried out following specific conditions, especially the management of waste disposed at the landfill sites.

d.   regulation of transportation of waste material, especially hazardous wastes.

e.   remedial action with regards to the rehabilitation of former landfill sites and cleaning up programmes.

Applying this to tourism means the need to innovate marketing and promotion campaigns and ensure that the distribution channels used promote the environmental qualities of the destinations and create a greater awareness of such resources. The design of the brochures will also assist in the process of ecological labelling of holidays. For example, images of long stretches of developed coastline immediately bring to mind a mass tourist resort, entertainment, noise, pollution, congestion, etc. Such images instill expectations and preconceptions about the resort which influence visitor behaviour. Eco-labelling can be introduced in brochures by including environmental information and concerns about the locality being visited, promoting the environmental qualities of tourist establishments and their programmes to improve their environmental performance, as well as 'awareness briefings ' to tourists prior to and during their holiday.

European Union legislation on waste obliges Member States to submit information regarding the implementation of the waste directive. This has been carried out through a questionnaire sent to Members States and which was to be returned by April 1995. The first report should be prepared by April 1996.

Tourism development creates various wastes e.g. construction/demolition waste, waste from food, paper, plastic, etc. On the Maltese Islands, most of this waste is disposed in the official landfill sites. However, even these sites are nearing full capacity and the disposal of waste is becoming a problem. A Solid Waste Management Strategy was prepared in 1993 identifying the medium and long-term actions to be taken to manage this problem. This will be done through prevention of waste production by introducing cleaner technology, sorting and recycling, implement advanced technology (e.g. incinerating), and provide safe landfill sites for the disposal of the remaining waste.

Earlier this year, the Government introduced a voluntary scheme whereby waste is sorted at source and specific days are allocated for the collection of the various wastes (organic and inorganic). The organic waste is then taken to the recycling plant. Although such a scheme has produced some results, the fact that it is voluntary does not encourage the public to separate its waste. Education and information should play a major role here with the general public being made aware of the reason for separating waste at the source, to be able to understand the problem and appreciate the efforts the Government is making. A recent statement by the minister concerned indicated that less than half of the waste is separated at source. Figures indicate that only 20% of the public were complying with this scheme.

The Environment Secretariat will be introducing a scheme designed to create new incentives for recycling, including the introduction of tipping charges at the island's main landfill site. A positive credit will be given to those bringing identified homogenous categories of waste to the landfill for recycling, whilst a debit note is issued to those bringing waste for disposal. As regards waste produced from catering establishments, this should be collected by a specific company at a fee. Unfortunately not all establishments comply with this regulation and place their waste together with the domestic waste, to be collected through the main waste collection system, thus avoiding the cost.

The tourism industry should make it one of its objectives to reduce waste and should also contribute to its disposal thus reducing the impacts of tourism development and activity. This should encourage self-regulation, especially in minimising the waste produced. A laissez-faire attitude will only create more harm and such an attitude would justify setting a price for waste collection.

The Canadian Restaurant and Foodservices Association produced an Environmental Guide for the Foodserve Industry entitled 'GOING GREEN without seeing red' (1992). With regards to waste management the recommendations include:

a) A waste audit to identify the quantity and type of waste (preferably par of an overall environmental audit),

b) Waste management to decide where, how and what waste can be reduced,

c) Implementing the plan through staff and customer involvement.

SEWAGE

Sewage becomes a serious pollutant if the quantity being disposed of is so high to slow down the natural biodegrading processes and therefore traces of raw sewage in the form of a plume can be seen on the water surface. It also results in pollution if the infrastructure is inadequate or does not cope with peak demand and, therefore, results in leakage or overflows, with sewage reaching the water table or bathing waters.

Only 30% of urban produced waste water from Mediterranean towns is given some form of treatment (World Bank/European Investment Bank, 1990). This means that 70% of the sewage effluent produced is flushed untreated into the sea, increasing bathing water pollution and also contributing to the loss of diversity as a result of the disturbance to the marine ecosystem.

The European Union has issued a Council Directive (91/271/EEC) regarding Urban Waste Water treatment. The Directive establishes a comprehensive system controlling the quality of urban waste water treatment and discharge from most population areas... It sets deadlines ranging from 31st December 1995 to 31st December 2005 for urban agglomerations of varying levels of population to provide collecting systems and at least secondary, biological treatment for urban waste water. (Commission of the European Communities, DG XI, 1992).

This makes it compulsory for Member States to invest in sewage treatment plants. The Maltese Island currently has only one treatment plant which handles about 20% of waste water produced. Another three sewage treatment plants are planned to be constructed in the near future, to abide with such regulations, considering that Malta has applied for EU membership, and considering that it is a signatory to the Barcelona Convention for the Protection of the Mediterranean Sea against Pollution. This will solve, to some extent, the problem of flushing untreated sewage into the sea. However, these plants will be constructed in natural coastal areas and will create other environmental impacts.

The Directive also refers to the re-use of treated waste water whenever appropriate, and subject to prior regulations and/or specific authorization. The Annex to this Directive includes the necessary parameters that have to be met and the sampling that is necessary before any treated waste water can be discharged from the treatment plant either to the sea or, especially, into sensitive areas. This is necessary to monitor and evaluate the results of treatment.

Pollution from sewage is closely related to the quality of water, especially bathing water. The quality of bathing water is very important for coastal tourism destinations and, therefore, tests are carried out to monitor whether such waters are within the maximum tolerable pollutant levels set by the European Union regulations of 1975 (76/160/EEC), and amended in 1994. The Directive specifies 19 physical, chemical and microbiological parameters for the quality of bathing water and establishes a system for the monitoring of bathing water quality by Member States. It is also the responsibility of the Member States to close these beaches which have pollutant concentrations higher than the tabulated values.

The quality of bathing water is important for coastal tourist destinations since polluted bathing waters may jeopardise the whole tourism sector in the locality. For example, the summer months of 1994 in the Maltese Islands were characterised by polluted beaches for the most part of the peak tourist months. This affected the tourism sector and increased the complaints.

Locals were also negatively affected by this situation because it was not possible to bathe on certain popular beaches. Such a situation came about as the result of a sewage system that was outdated and unable to meet the current demands. Works were undertaken in 1995 to improve the situation in the main tourist areas and the problem did not recur this summer.

The Environmental Protection Act of Malta of 1992, provides the basis for the protection of the environment of Malta from sewage pollution in various sections of the Act. This Act specifies that no substance should be discharged into the sea except where it has been verified that the substance to be discharged will not endanger human or animal health and will not be a threat to the marine environment. In granting a permit to discharge substances, it is necessary to provide specific information particularly with regards to the nature and quantity of the substance disposed, frequency, method of discharge and the site where the substance is to be discharged. All kinds of effluents require a permit, with a few exceptions, for example, discharges related to ships, platforms and aircrafts.

It is mandatory to carry out an environmental impact assessment for those developments concerned with the disposal of wastes, e.g. treatment plants, depositing of sludge.

Fines and other penalties are imposed on those who do not abide by the regulations and through malice, negligence or non-observance of the regulations create some damage to the environment. Such penalties also include the confiscation of the equipment that has caused the damage.

The Minister responsible for the Environment is to establish systems of control of the quality of the environment, to collect and publish data, to study and monitor changes of ecological systems and to order research to be conducted and studies to be made regarding environmental pollution. The monitoring of bathing water quality is carried out between the Ministry for the Environment (Environment Secretariat) and the Department of Health.

Legislation with regards to the monitoring of the bathing water quality, although necessary, has its limitations. The EU Directive does not specify when the sampling has be made. Thus, it is possible for localities to carry out the sampling early in the morning when the water would be relatively clean. Taking samples later in the day, when activity on the beach is at its peak would certainly give different results. It is also possible for areas to conceal their findings to avoid embarrassment from the tourist sector and to maintain a positive image of the resort.

Large hotels worldwide are taking the responsibility to treat the sewage created as a result of their operations and using the secondary water for irrigation purposes. New hotel developments of a certain scale should be encouraged to install small treatment plants and re-use the water, especially in those destinations where water is scarce.

The treatment of sewage results in a sludge residue. On the Maltese Islands, the disposal of this sludge into the sea will stop by 1998 and this will be turned into a compost at the solid waste recycling plant. Such plants are located in the vicinity of residential areas and, on more than one occasion, the local residents protested to the authorities because of the odours emitted from the plant.

The Sewage Master Plan for the Maltese Islands, referred to above, recommends that three sewage treatment plants be constructed at the main outfulls.

The disposal of raw sewage into the sea, especially where lakes are concerned, results in the eutrophication of lakes, since nutrients are increased substantially. This will accelerate the growth of algae which disturbs the balance of organisms present in the water and degrades water quality (EC Council, 1991). Such disposal may also result in the decline of certain species while encouraging the increase of opportunistic species. Thus the whole marine ecosystem experiences a radical change. For example, the proliferation of opportunistic epiphytic algae cuts off the supply of sunlight to a very important sea grass named *Posodonia oceanica*, which is therefore indirectly affected by pollution. This leads to a decline in the species supported by this sea grass (Camilleri, 1994).

It is in the interest of the authorities to place warning signs in those bathing areas affected by pollution. Unfortunately, this is not always the case. Very often such notices are removed form the beaches in Malta as soon as they are put up, while some

British local authorities are reluctant to publicise low quality bathing waters. (Walker, 1992).

OTHER FORMS OF POLLUTION AS A RESULT OF TOURIST ACTIVITY

Tourist activity is liable to cause other forms of pollution, unless such activity is appropriately managed and planned. Air pollution is created as a result of heavy traffic moving into the countryside or in historic urban centres. Emissions from vehicles into the air pollute the natural environment leaving its effects on the flora and fauna while in the historic city centres such emissions are affecting building facades. European Community policy in this field encourages the use of lead-free petrol and catalytic converters to reduce the level of pollutants contained in vehicle exhaust gases.

Noise pollution is another problem resulting from heavy traffic, entertainment establishments, crowds, bars, etc. Such problems can be solved through responsible behaviour and through the use of sound-proof material in construction.

One of the main "pollutions" attributed to tourism development is that of visual pollution. The unsightly constructions that have been built along coastal areas have completely altered the characteristics of the locality, bringing in alien forms of architecture which is not sensitive to the scale and environment of the locality. Small fishing villages turn into tourist resorts, bringing drastic changes to the quality of the life led by the residents. Careful design which respects the surrounding environment and the scale of the locality would lead to more sensitive developments, tailored for the areas rather than being imposed.

Yachting is another popular tourism activity. Studies carried out in Malta on a particular species of snail have shown that the use of antifouling paints has resulted in an abnormality known technically as imposex. Female snails affected by imposex develop male sex organs as a result of such pollution. The use of TBT in the antifouling paints is being controlled since studies have indicated that its use has serious effects on the ecology and may have serious effects on humans, even though the impact on humans has not yet been studied.

Finally, tourist development has also contributed to what can be termed as 'social pollution'. Behavioural patterns of tourists have brought changes to the local communities of various destination in customs, traditions and values. Such form of pollution is long-term and becomes evident after years of development. It is therefore important to be aware that such changes are occurring and should be monitored through continuous research with the local communities.

CONCLUSION

Tourism activity if planned and managed in a sensitive way based on the principles of ensuring a sustainable development, will certainly reduce the level of pollution it creates. However, the introduction of legislation, although important, will solve only part of the problem. Legislation needs enforcement to ensure compliance with the law and action taken when compliance is lacking. Voluntary action through a sense of self-responsibility from those operating in the sector should ensure a more effective instrument to reduce pollution. After all, having a well-kept environment benefits tourism in the end.

COASTAL CONSERVATION: IMPACT OF TOURISM ON NATURAL BIOTOPES

Louis BRIGAND
Lecturer in Geography, University
of Western Brittany, France

The growth of human pressure on coastal areas is a striking development which affects all continents. France enjoys a highly privileged geographical position, being one of the European countries most richly endowed with coastlines. These marine areas extend over the shores of the Channel, the Atlantic and the Mediterranean, a feature which has now become a major economic development asset, most of all for tourism in that the coasts are ideal holiday destinations.

This interest in the coast is actually quite recent. The most radical changes, particularly in the realm of tourism, made their appearance during this century. Until then, the coastal environment was not perceived as it is today but regarded as forbidding and inhospitable. As a result, coastal settlement was relatively sparse, clustering in a few precise geographical locations singled out for the quality of their harbour sites.

In the space of a century the coasts underwent major changes to become a singularly coveted environment. Maritime trade expanded, thus considerably increasing the extent of the ports. Industrial activities became concentrated near these port complexes. Last and not least of the developments which occurred, tourist activities were attracted to the coasts in a big way. A place where residence used to be dictated by pure necessity last century has become the most coveted of all. The consequences of this new interest are by no means secondary.

The coast has thus become a location in great demand for varied and often competing activities. The pressure of urbanisation has subjected its natural biotopes to an astounding evolution, in that they are increasingly rare as well as popular. Meanwhile new recreational functions have been defined for them, different uses have emerged, and conservation standards and development patterns have been devised.

This raises genuine difficulties for the management of these coastal habitats. As such they have no intrinsic economic value, but considerably more as eligible building land! On the other hand, they are generally areas of extreme ecological fragility visited by ever larger numbers of city-dwellers avidly seeking nature and the open air. For their management and development, it is thus imperative to assess their environmental sensitivity along with their ability to absorb ever-increasing human pressure.

1. Impact of tourism on natural biotopes

A coastal biotope remains a relative concept. Few coastal areas are unexploited by man; until comparatively recent times, all were used for a variety of purposes. Even the most outlying and inaccessible sites such as islands and islets were turned to account, some being used to run livestock, others for mining. Admittedly most of these activities were "low-impact", but their impact was not entirely negligible. Sand-dunes, for instance, were used for sand-quarrying, grazing or drying seaweed. In wetlands, rushes and reeds were harvested and hunting was carried on. Each type of environment had corresponding forms of exploitation which have now largely given way to other more modern uses. Many of these have a direct relationship with tourist trade interests.

Tourism has established itself as a predominant activity in just a few decades. It is the leading sector of the economy in France, which has become a major European tourist destination. Every aspect of the economy and society is influenced. It is present in most regions, but especially by the waterside. The environmental repercussions raise a great many questions. Tourism, with its multiple forms, major consequences and openness to the world, is asserting itself more and more as an inescapable reality, vital to the future of certain coastal areas and of the resident populations which depend on it for their livelihood.

The effects of tourism development on natural biotopes are in direct correlation with the forms of tourism; accordingly, the repercussions may be either very small or enormous. It is in fact possible to measure the impact according to an artificialisation criterion. The greater the artificialisation of a locality, the more significant the impact of tourism on nature. Thus the construction of mammoth hotel complexes, golf links or marinas has highly devastating effects on the natural habitats along the coast, which are often irreparably destroyed by projects of this kind. Conversely, nature tourism in connection with rambling, for instance, has a lower impact. Nonetheless, in some instances the tourist carrying capacity of certain locations is exceeded and thus calls for specific planning measures. This is the case with the tracts of sand dunes or coastal heath severely damaged by trampling due to the high visiting rate.

The inroads associated with the presence of a tourist population are thus multifarious: effluent, refuse, uncontrolled or organised urbanisation, disturbance of animal and plant populations, destruction and standardisation of habitats, and disordered consumption of natural space. The present concern is therefore to minimise these ill-effects and above all to preserve and protect certain sites hitherto untouched by urbanisation. This policy is bound to develop with the increasingly noticeable trend of fashion towards discovery of high-quality nature areas. Such being the outlook, it can be propounded that tourism is also conducive to appreciation of the value of a site and may even result in its protection and possibly restoration. This is the idea behind the extensive operation being conducted by the Autonomous Government of the Balearic Islands to reclaim the coastal sites of certain islands, for instance on Mallorca where excessive urbanisation had caused a decline in tourist traffic.

It is now realised that the attractiveness of a landscape is linked with its quality, so that the value given to the countryside determines the level of tourist potential. It is well-known that measures to protect and classify certain sites as parks or reserves raise growing interest among visitors and generate new problems of public access. The question of the impact of tourism on natural habitats is seen to be complex.

In the final analysis, efforts must centre on discovering new forms of sustainable tourism development which will reconcile often divergent interests and lead to innovative land-use practices. The idea is in fact to discover forms of conservation which remain acceptable to people and ecosystems alike. This calls for very serious consideration of the entry and visiting conditions applying to coastal nature spots.

2.   Protection of coastal biotopes: an indispensable prerequisite

Awareness of the need to protect these areas is comparatively recent in France, dating from the 1970s. Before then, nature reserves and a legislative framework already existed. In practice, however, few areas were genuinely protected and large expanses of coastal land still in a natural state had been finally and irreversibly given over to urbanisation before that time. This was especially true of the Mediterranean coasts. The process was not peculiar to France and also occurred in Spain (Costa Brava; Costa del Sol).

Since then the legislation has been significantly strengthened and toughened. There is now a complex scale of protection status allowing numerous problems to be addressed. The variety and superimposition of laws in force reflects the highly significant issues affecting the coast. There is no need for a tiresome recital of the legislative instruments relating to biotope conservation; let us simply try to distinguish their most fundamental aspects.

These protective instruments serve various purposes. One instance is the nature reserves whose purpose is strictly to preserve areas of major environmental value. Human presence in these nature reserves is stringently controlled. There are several types of reserve allowing more ready public access. Other protection techniques have a more structural quality and a more direct relationship with the control of urbanisation, eg the classified sectors and the non-building areas marked on the land-use plans. Still other forms of protection employ demarcation of zones in an effort to reconcile sustainable development and preservation of natural space. Such are the biosphere reserves whose general intent is preservation of biological diversity, rural development and scientific research, under constant surveillance. These are in fact non-standard protected areas created under flexible arrangements and adapted to the local ecological and socio-economic conditions.

These instruments ensure more or less strict protection of natural habitats but do not settle the important question of their management. Protection entails the finding of solutions to ensure firm protection, preserve natural balance and control human presence. For some years there has been a profusion of management plans aimed at programming and directing the evolution of protected areas on the basis of certain priorities.

To end this brief overview of conservation methods, mention should be made of land purchase. This remains the most conclusive means of protection against the greed of property developers, since bought-up areas are permanently preserved from risks of urbanisation. At present the local authorities and in particular the "départements" are acquiring coastal land with funds derived from a tax levied on all new building projects. But the biggest operator in this sector is undoubtedly the Conservancy for Coasts and Lake Shores (Conservatoire de l'Espace du Littoral et des Rivages Lacustres).

3.   The Conservancy for Coasts: an original agency serving the conservation and human use of nature

The Conservancy, a government-run public institution, was established under the Act of 10 July 1975. Its task is to purchase nature areas under threat of degradation and destruction and to preserve them with their full diversity and wealth for future generations. Its sphere of competence extends over the coastal districts of the French mainland and overseas "départements", as well as municipalities beside lakes and inland waters with an area of 1,000 hectares or more.

The Conservancy's action over the past 20 years has been highly significant. On 1 January 1995 it owned 334 sites totalling 44,334 hectares and taking in 622 km of shoreline, ie 10% of the entire French coast. This body, organised in regional units, is staffed by over 50 persons and operates with state financial support. As a foundation for the coasts in the truest sense, it is authorised in addition to receive donations and bequests. The Conservancy also carries out important scientific information work by organising quarterly colloquies and publishing frequent issues in the series *Les Cahiers du Conservatoire*. All these activities are placed in a long-term context.

While the Conservancy's top priority is to arrange the purchase of threatened nature areas, it also answers for their quality. In order to achieve its aims, it enters into partnerships with local authorities not only for its purchasing programme but also as regards the management plans. The Conservancy itself does not manage the sites in its possession; instead, it concludes management agreements with the local authorities or with suitably qualified associations. Its ultimate aim is to control one-third of the French coasts, as it already does in Corsica.

The Conservancy for Coasts will plainly be designated to perform a growing role in French coastal conservation policy. Through its schemes to purchase and rehabilitate coastal sites and control public access to them, the Conservancy has gained a great deal of experience which has been shared, in Europe, by the century-old British National Trust. Because of the lasting surety which this type of structure offers for coastal nature conservation and management, in the near future it could be the focus of renewed interest in the coasts of Europe; the Conservancy, furthermore, has already set up appropriate contacts with other states, Tunisia in particular.

CONTROL OF TOURIST DEVELOPMENT LIABLE TO HAVE SIGNIFICANT CONSEQUENCES ON THE ENVIRONMENT: NATIONAL, REGIONAL AND LOCAL PLANNING POLICY

Anthony Ellul
Malta

INTRODUCTION

The use of the word 'controls' in the tourism sector is very often met with some degree of opposition or suspicion, particularly from the private sector operating the tourism sector. The development of tourism in various destinations (e.g. Spain, Greece, Bali, Turkey, Malta) has been characterised by a "laisser-faire" approach to development, dominated by the private sector and which was strongly dependent on market demand. Market forces shaped tourism development. The economic opportunities which tourism development offered were attractive, many countries jumped on the bandwagon and developed a tourism industry to satisfy the increasing demand from tour operators for more beds. Various destinations became the fashion of the day and what were once simple coastal villages were turned into extensive seaside resorts, displacing the previous activities and opening them up to the tourist 'hoards'.

Tourism is a complex phenomenon and research concerning such an activity, especially with regard to its impact and planning approaches, is quite recent. Thus, any reflections on past tourism development must be made bearing this in mind. On the other hand, such experiences should provide the stimulus for new developing destinations to seek a more environmentally compatible tourism development.

Tourism development is mainly the result of private sector initiatives. Government's role in tourism development is usually concerned with the planning and marketing functions, overseeing that standards are maintained, and ensuring an adequate infrastructure. The private sector provides the necessary tourism superstructure (hotels, restaurants, attractions, tour programmes) and also seeks to maximize their returns on investment. Therefore, any control of tourism development will be perceived as some form of threat to their investment opportunities. Past approaches to development have created a tourism culture among the private sector and also among tourism authorities. This sometimes makes it rather difficult to look for other approaches.

Certainly, there are various initiatives, taken particularly by big hotel chains and some by the large tour operators, to integrate environmental safeguards in their operations. Yet, tourism is a sector dominated by the small entrepreneur and therefore change becomes somewhat slow to materialise. Nonetheless, such change is necessary to restore the positive image tourism deserves, an image which has been tarnished as a result of bad planning and management of tourism and their functions. New measures must be identified to develop tourism in a more managed and planned approach.

DEFINITIONS

Before proceeding further, it is important to point out at this stage that controls should not be understood as some measure to stop development, but is defined as a set of instruments that would shape and direct the sustainable development of tourism. Therefore, instruments that should promote tourism development that:

- respects and conserves the natural, cultural and social heritage;
- does not jeopardise the quality of life of the local community;
- offers tourists a satisfactory experience and one of quality;
- provides the investor with an adequate return on investment.

Controls should therefore be seen as leading to the improvement of the environmental performance of tourism planning and development, rather than restrained development.

The other important phrase in the title of this paper is tourism development. Tourism development should not be limited to structural developments, constructions and buildings, but also to tourism activity which includes tours, walking, bathing, sightseeing and many other activities carried out by tourists. Even such activities, if not managed in the appropriate way are liable to cause a negative impact on the environment. Assessment of tourism projects is very often limited to an assessment of the structure being built and rarely includes an assessment of the activities that will result from such development. Hence, this includes the relationships with the local community and visits to historical and natural sites.

The final term which needs some explanation is 'significant consequences'. Without doubt, tourism development creates a level of impact. However, such influences can be immediate, for example the complete destruction of an ecological fragile area, or gradual, for example changes in values, lifestyles, customs and changes in the dynamic processes of nature. Assessment of tourism development has concentrated very much on the former, with little attention being given to the likely future impact of a particular development.

Therefore, by introducing controls in the sector this certainly does not mean that the development of tourism will be completely checked and stopped. On the other hand, this should offer the opportunity to reflect on tourism development and seek to establish new measures aimed at better management of the sector and to develop a new tourism philosophy among the various players to achieve the sustainable development of tourism activity.

CONTROL INSTRUMENTS

Control instruments can be introduced in various forms which can be grouped under the following six categories:

- Planning policy
- Legislation
- Economic
- Information
- Organisation
- Voluntary

An examination of the various control instruments within each category follows.

PLANNING POLICY

The need for planning tourism development, as a reaction to the early approaches to tourism development has only been felt over the last two decades. 'At a tourism seminar in Yugoslavia in 1972, Dr. Dresa Car, Deputy President, Republican Council for Tourism, summed up the attitude of that period: "Is planning necessary? Is planning possible? We don't know how to plan for tourism." But even at that time, others were showing that tourism planning was necessary and possible.' (Gunn, 1988).

A document prepared by the WTO in 1978 called *Inventory of Tourist Development Plans*, summarised the results from a survey of about 118 national tourism administrations. Thirty-seven nations responded and out of these, 'twenty-six stated that they had a plan under way, eight replied that a plan was in preparation, and three said that there was both a plan under way and in preparation.' (Gunn, 1988). The reasons given by *Baud-Bovy* (1982) as to why few plans were implemented were various. Plans generally encouraged land speculation, plans were not easily adapted to changing situations and little attention was given to the mechanism of the tourism sector, the structures of the industry and the integrated approach to tourism development.

Tourism planning has to take place at three levels. At the national and regional levels 'planning is concerned with tourism development policies, structure plans, facility standards, institutional factors and all other elements necessary to develop and manage tourism. Then within the framework of national and regional planning, more detailed plans for tourist attractions, resort, urban, rural and other forms of tourism development can be prepared'. (Inskeep, 1994). The latter would be at the local or site planning level.

Planning is the most effective control of tourism development. It establishes the overall objectives, strategies and policies for tourism development and when environmental concerns are embedded into the planning framework then the environmental planning approach provides the basis for the sustainable development of tourism. The Environmental Planning Approach technique involves surveying and analysing all environmental resources and basing decisions on the appropriate type and location of development on such an analysis. In this way intensive development would not be permitted in those areas where it would result in a loss of environmental resources. Such an approach is also based on a community approach to tourism development, which involves the community in the planning and development of types of tourism that would benefit the local residents.

An environmentally-based Planning Model is presented by *Ross Dowling*. The model presented is based on environmental conservation and seeks to promote an environmentally compatible sustainable tourism development. The significant aspect of this model is that tourism development is planned following an evaluation of environmental resources and especially the local community. 'The uniqueness of the EBT regional planning model lies in its environmental base, incorporation of both resident and tourist opinions, its functional differentiation in order to achieve environment-tourism compatibility and its provision of a new approach to sustainable tourism planning'. (Dowling, 1993).

In this model, the strategies and controls follow the survey and evaluation stages. The survey of both environmental attributes and tourism resources leads to the determination of the significant features, by incorporating in the plan the views and opinions of tourists and locals on which resources should be developed for tourism. Thus critical areas or areas of conflict and compatible activities are identified, which will then lead to the identification of strategic policies and controls for the proposed developments and activities. Such policies and controls may be related to zoning of areas for development or for protection as well as direct (charges, regulations) and indirect (interpretation, education) management options.

Tourism planning should be integrated with planning in other sectors of the economy to avoid conflicts of interest and the over-use of resources. Tourism activity does not develop in isolation, but is dependent on other activities, and therefore to ensure an integrated development approach to tourism development, tourism planning policies must relate to planning policies in other sectors and vice-versa. In this way any conflicts between the various development sectors will be minimised and pressure on the scarce resources reduced.

The zoning technique is a very effective land use control, particularly in developing tourism resorts. Through such a technique, tourism development is allocated to appropriate areas and protected areas are 'zoned off' from development. Land usage in such zones is specified and clearly defined standards for tourism development will apply in such zones. Structure Plans usually identify such zones and recommend Development Briefs for the zones which would 'prescribe' the specific standards of tourism development in the area. Developers will have to adhere to these standards.

In Denmark, for example, a new 3 km coastal planning zone imposes strong restrictions on tourist development on open coastlines. However, such a process should not isolate tourism from other sectors of development, especially with regards to competition for the factors of production (e.g. capital and labour). Secondly, tourist activity is not only restricted to such areas. Tourists explore and seek experiences outside the resort areas and therefore the extent and intensity of development in the zone will influence the nearby areas.

On the other hand, the scale and type of tourism development, especially in new areas, should reflect the character, needs, capacities and aspirations of the local population and their environment. It is the locality that should determine the scale and type of tourism development rather than the other way round, as has been the case with many Mediterranean resorts. *Inskeep* refers to 'carrying capacity analysis' as a methodology which provides guidelines in establishing the type and scale of development in an area (Inskeep, 1994). Such an analysis identifies the limits and constraints that will determine the level of development appropriate to the site to ensure the protection and conservation of the cultural and ecological resources. Such constraints may include residents' toleration levels, areas to be protected because of their ecological, archaeological or scientific value, tourists' satisfaction levels, infrastructural provisions, etc. Tourism planning policies will have to reflect these concerns and propose appropriate policies in this respect.

Planning at the local level should reflect the policies set out at the national and regional levels. Planning at the local level could be considered as the actual implementation of the previous planning levels which would be more of a generic nature. This vertical integration maintains a link between all levels of planning. The national policies are translated into regional policies and these in turn into more detailed site-oriented local policies. Having clear environmentally-based policies directing the development of tourism is at the foundation of a planned tourism development, and would provide strategic controls for tourism development.

Planning permission for major tourism projects should be subject to a consultation process that involves other sectors of the economy and the local community. Public consultation, although not an easy process, is necessary, and in the case of large developments, such consultation should start at the early stages of the planning process. In this way the scale of the project would be designed to take into account the needs and requirements of the local community. Public consultation is a very difficult process since to be successful and effective the consulted public should be informed so as to be in a position to decide - otherwise public consultation will turn out to be a political battle rather than a situation where there is a positive discussion to achieve a sustainable development.

From a national economic development aspect it is important to define the role tourism should play in the future. In the economic sense, tourism will compete with other sectors for scarce resources and therefore, it becomes more important to define the role of tourism in the national economy and its relation to other development sectors. Various tourist destinations have created an economic dependence on tourism and this dependence brings about various economic problems during times of crisis. Therefore, tourism development must be seen within the overall economic development plan and not in isolation in order to avoid an economic over-dependence on a particular sector. This is also important when allocating resources to ensure their optimal allocation, especially infrastructure. In the long term, problems may arise if one sector has benefited from the provision of infrastructure at the expense of other development sectors.

LEGISLATION

The introduction of legislation is another form of control. There are few examples of specific legislation on tourism and the environment. Generally, environmental legislation is not specific to one sector but looks at the protection of the environment from all development sectors and from all possible threats. There are however some examples.

The Republic of Croatia has introduced a law on Tourism Communities and Promotion of Tourism in Croatia to enhance public awareness of the problems relating to the preservation and rehabilitation of the cultural and historic monuments and environmental protection through tourism organisations.

On the Maltese Islands two important laws have been introduced in recent years with the aim of conserving the environment. The Development Planning Act of 1992 is the Act regulating development and identifies those developments that require a development permit as well as establishing the process to be followed in the development control process. This legislation has also set up the Planning Authority - the institution responsible for all planning related to land use the conservation of the environment.

The second important piece of legislation is the Environment Protection Act of 1992. This Act is the main law regarding the protection of the natural environment from pollution, development and other activities that may cause harm to the environmental resources. Other countries also have their own laws with regards to environmental protection.

The Republic of Latvia has a number of laws including one on Environmental Protection, on Particularly Protected Nature Areas, Protected Belts and the Regulation on Physical Planning and Building. Norway has the Planning and Building Act (1978), the Nature Conservation Act (1970), the Cultural Heritage Act (1978) and the Pollution Control Act (1981). Various other countries have enacted their own legislation relating to protecting nature areas, controlling pollution and development control.

The European Union has also adopted various types of legislation regarding the environment. The European Union can issue **directives** to the Member States which must be reflected in the laws or regulations of the Members States within a designated time limit, or **recommendations** which do not bind the Member States. One important recommendation is the one regarding the Polluter Pays Principle. This states that anyone 'responsible for pollution must pay the costs of such measures as are necessary to eliminate that pollution so to reduce it, so as to comply with the standard or equivalent measures laid down by the authorities'. (EEC, 1992). Although this principle is another form of control that would encourage developers to take all the necessary precautions to avoid polluting and then having to pay for its elimination, the directive on Environmental Impact Assessment embodies more the preventive approach rather than the remedial. This Directive lists those developments which require an EIA, many tourism projects do, but not all.

All tourism developments should be subject to a level of impact assessment. Tourism development generates activity which in itself will create an impact that is probably far greater than the development itself. On the Maltese Islands, for example, only new tourist accommodation developments, of over sixty beds, require some form of impact assessment; this excludes those projects which request an extension. Yet, such projects are certainly creating a level of impact and this should be assessed. Impact assessments are to be extended to policies and plans and not just to individual projects as it is the case at present. Policies and plans should be assessed with regards to their effectiveness in protecting the environment.

Environmental Impact Assessments have become a statutory requirement in many countries. Such an assessment would identify those aspects of a project likely to cause harm to the environment and the degree of such harm. It would also suggest mitigation measures, where possible, to reduce the project's impact through alterations in the scheme being proposed.

EIA's with regard to tourism however, are mainly concerned with examining the project's impact on the natural and social environments. The impact on the economic environment of tourism projects and the impact on tourism itself is rarely considered when terms of reference for the preparation of an EIA for tourism development are being drawn up. Certainly the environment must be protected, yet should not tourism be protected from itself? A number of projects were allowed to develop in various destinations (Mallorca, Costa del Sol, Malta) which after some years, experienced a decline in their economic well-being. This decreases the standards adopted by the establishment and makes it more vulnerable to the demands of our competitors. The tourism concept of many projects was designed to achieve short-term results and in the long term they lost competitivity, thus, they could not be economically sustainable. The tourism product also changed. What once attracted an 'elite' type of tourist, opened its doors to the masses and lost its inherent attraction. In this sense, it is necessary to protect tourism from tourism development. Planning, as explained above, plays an important role.

Enacting legislation however, although important and necessary, will not work unless there is proper law enforcement. This will entail the appropriate management structures monitoring and policing. Enforcement is not an easy task and its implementation varies from country to country depending on the prevailing environmental culture. In those countries where it is strong, the community itself would enforce the legislation. In countries where such a culture is rather weak, government structures would be necessary to ensure enforcement.

ECONOMIC

Economic controls can come in two forms - incentives or taxes. Various countries have introduced diverse incentive packages to assist the development of tourism. Such incentives come in the form of grants, soft loans, tax holidays, exemptions from customs duties, etc. Incentives have been a major tool in encouraging investment in tourism development. However, incentives have another important role to play; incentive packages should be designed to reflect planning policies. Special incentive packages should be provided to encourage the appropriate type of development in the appropriate locality and to encourage investment in specific sectors of the tourism industry, especially in product development.

Canada, for example, offers a Regional Aid Incentive Programme specific to particular regions which includes loans, grants, planning assistance, feasibility studies, and contributions to marketing and promotion. **Greece** also offers Preferential Grants for 'special investments' including the rehabilitation of traditional buildings to be used as hostels, hotel facilities or workshops for traditional handicrafts. **Portugal** makes grants available for certain events promoting culture and artistic activities. In **the UK**, Urban Development Grants are available to promote the economic and physical regeneration of inner urban areas, by encouraging private sector investment into such areas.

Taxes, on the other hand, are introduced to discourage development or activities that would have an adverse impact on the environment; the 'polluter pays' principle, mentioned above, is one such a tax. There are however both advantages and disadvantages to the tax approach.

In Malta, catering and tourist establishments pay a fee to a private company for the collection of their waste, even though not all establishments abide this practice. Taxes are often introduced for specific sectors to encourage waste management, reduction of emissions and treatment of sewage. Forms of taxes directly related to tourism include charging relatively high admission prices in areas which are fragile and sensitive, in order to limit visitor numbers and charging higher than normal commercial rates for electricity and water consumption in tourist establishments.

Environmental costs should also be integrated into the project assessment process. Environmental resources are not infinite, and therefore the depletion of resources has a cost attached. Very often such costs are not taken into consideration. Certainly, some costs would be difficult to quantify, nonetheless, some form of provision in the cost/benefit analysis of any project should be made to cater for the cost of this loss of resources.

INFORMATION

Planning would not be possible without the availability of the right information. Information is another important aspect in controlling development. Information can be obtained through surveys, tests, data collection, exchange of experiences and various other forms of research.

Environmental indicators are also being studied in a process to develop indicators of environmental performance, WTO has been studying such indicators which, if implemented, would shed light on the sustainable development of tourism. Such indicators will provide the monitoring of the impact relation to tourism development and would include indicators on social stress, ecological and cultural degradation, tourist satisfaction, economic strength and utilisation of resources, among others.

Surveys and tests are also necessary. Surveys to record changing attitudes of the local community towards tourism development and tests as regards the quality of bathing waters are just two examples of the type of information necessary to monitor tourism development, and to identify changes which would be reflected in the updating of planning policies.

Awareness programmes, can be perceived by locals and tourists, as a form of control. Codes of conduct for both tourists and locals and the tourism sector, serve to create a greater awareness on the opportunities of environmental protection. Various good practice guides have been developed by hotels chains (International Hotels Environment Programme initiative), theme parks and automobile clubs. UNEP has published a report in its technical series, which focused on Environmental Codes of Conduct for Tourism. Certainly, there are quite a few in hand. Codes in action oriented and should be the result of a collective effort and contribution from all actors in the tourism sector - private, public and the local community, as well as with tourists.

Interpretation of natural and cultural heritage is an activity which brings the meaning of such resources to the general public and the tourist in a form that is both educational and entertaining. Interpretation not only concerns the provision of information, but also takes an additional role in the area of visitor management. Besides informing visitors about the resource and its attributes, it serves to control and manage visitor movement around a site, thus causing minimal negative impact to the resource.

ORGANISATION

None of the above measures can be effectively implemented unless there is an appropriate organisation to manage and oversee the tourism sector. This organisation includes both the public and private sectors since no sustainable tourism development can be achieved without the partnership and collaboration between these two sectors.

The appropriate public sector arrangement is necessary to ensure a well-planned and managed tourism development. Such a set up should be given equal importance to planning and marketing even though, in most cases, the latter has taken precedence. In addition to these two functions, the monitoring of standards on quality is another important public sector role.

Private sector organisations should also increase their involvement in environmental issues and encourage their members to adopt environmentally compatible operations. Strong links between the private and public sector are very often reflected in the National Tourist Boards which are usually composed of members from both sectors. Such organisations are to be equipped with trained personnel in the various specialisations. Tourism involves a multi-disciplinary approach to development and therefore an array of professionals in diverse fields will have to be involved. The establishment of training programmes and training institutions to meet the needs of the sector should be multi-faceted in their approach to design training packages.

Tourism organisations should also establish links with other sectors to ensure involvement of other parties in tourism development, increasing awareness of the sector and develop coordinated policies in developing tourism and its relations with other development sectors.

Local authorities are the implementing bodies of policies and plans and should have the necessary expertise to direct tourism development. Such authorities should be at the forefront in developing awareness campaigns among local communities to foster a positive tourism culture that respects the environment and its resources, and offers tourists a satisfactory experience.

VOLUNTARY

Finally, I wish to mention some controls that can be implemented on a voluntary basis at projet level. The IHEP is a voluntary initiative taken up by the major hotel chains in implementing measures regarding aspects of sewage treatment, water conservation, energy conservation, waste management and pollution control. The International Hotel Environment Initiative (IHEP) is a programme supported by the major hotel chains which have committed themselves to sustainable tourism development and are seeking practical measures to implement the concept.

Tourist developments should be encouraged to carry out environmental audits. Such audits should assess the environmental performance of the establishment and should help in directing the establishment's operations towards a greater environmental concern. This will not only give long term economical return to the establishment, but will also ensure that the activity is monitored as regards the impact it creates on the environment, and propose mitigation measures to improve the environmental performance of key operations.

The planning of marketing and promotional campaigns also plays an important role in the protection of the environment. Very often demand factors predominated marketing campaigns, and little thought was given to the supply side. Thus, this resulted in attracting markets which, in the long term, created pressure on the destination's environmental resources. Market and product mismatch is dangerous, and could harm the tourism industry. Marketing campaigns should reflect and be based on the product available. A problem with many Mediterranean destinations that promote and market their cultural and historic assets, is that resources do not have the appropriate management structures and the presentation of such resources leaves much to be desired. Therefore, attracting visitors to such sites will increase the potential damage, as a result of a lack of visitor management, and will also offer a negative visitor experience of the visitor. The result of this will be visitor dissatisfaction. Thus marketing should evolve with product development.

Partnerships between the private and public sector is another form of control which should aim at developing tourism as a gradual process, especially if this should be complemented with a satisfactory level of infrastructure and manpower requirements. The latter takes time to develop and the experience in other destinations, in the past has shown that were tourism development created pressures on the infrastructure and where the supply of trained personnel did not match demand, the tourism sector faced serious problems.

As regards training, partnerships have developed between Central, Eastern and Western European national parks, such as between Sumava in Bohemia and Bayerischer Wald in Germany and between Ojcow in Poland and the Peak District in the UK. Initiatives like the 'Walled Town Friendship Circle' which bring together some one hundred and nine towns in fifteen countries, have resulted not only in the exchange of experience between towns, but also in the production of a manual entitled 'A Handbook of Good practice for Sustainable Tourism in Walled Towns'.

International organisations, particularly the Council of Europe and the European Union, are providing through their work assistance to the Central and Eastern European countries in various forms, be it financial (e.g. Phare Programme of the EU) or through technical assistance of which this Colloquy is the proof. Such tools provide the opportunity for a better understanding of the tourism sector and lead the way for the appropriate management and planning of the sector, and also prove the financial means to realise the various projects.

CONCLUSION

The above is just a brief overview of various measures that could assist in ensuring an environmentally compatible tourism development. Certainly, there are other measures which can be discussed, in particular limiting bed supply and other measures to limit tourist numbers in certain localities, and means to ease tourism pressures as has been carried out in Mallorca to remove 25,000 bed spaces.

I hope that this presentation has been thought-provoking, and possibly there would be an opportunity, during the discussion session, to expand and discuss further some of the points presented.

THE CASE OF ALBANIA

Arch. Genc METOHU
Head of Tourism Regional Projects Sector
Ministry of Construction and Tourism, Albania

A brief overview of the real possibilities in implementing a tourism development strategy in Albania: one in harmony with the political solution of land ownership as repayment to the former owners of agricultural and construction land and the privatisation of land, environmental policy and the perspective development policy of Albanian society.

From 1992, with the favourable political conditions, Albania has become a new tourist destination in Europe providing a unique opportunity for the development of tourism in full harmony with the natural and human environment. The country's nature and ecology allow for the possible development of all kinds of tourism. Albania now has an ideal opportunity to become Europe's leading eco-tourism destination, with an image of a safe environment, unpolluted by the tourist. The unspoilt coasts, in particular, must be preserved; we will allow low buildings, in general, of 1-2 storeys which blend well with the surrounding environment. The conception and compilation of the tourism development strategy and the policies that will be implemented for this purpose are aimed at realising long-term tourism in harmony with the environment in our country.

From this standpoint, the development of tourism in Albania can be broken down into the following areas:

- Adriatic coastal resorts and marinas;
- Ionic coastal resorts and marinas;
- mountain resorts;
- lakeside resorts (along the Ohrid, Shkodra and Prespa lakes).

Albania may have the smallest and most undeveloped Mediterranean coastline compared to the other countries, approximately 450 km. Its Adriatic coastline is 284 km in length and is characteristic for its heterogenous combination of ecosystems such as the delta of rivers Buna, Drini, Mati, Ishmi, Erzeni, Shkumbini, Semani, Vjosa; lagoons in the form of a chain from the north: Viluni, Kenalle, Merxhani-Kunea-Vaini, Patok, Karavasta, Narta, Pasha Liman and wetlands such as Rrushkulli, etc; sand dunes, for example Psho Poro; woodlands; forests such as 'Divjaka Pine', etc, and some wide beaches with fine sand, a seaside in transition due to the accumulative process of the river deltas. The Ionic coast, 154 km in length, is rocky and with clean water.

For this reason a legal network compiled a Law for "Priority Tourism Development Zones", "The strategy of tourism development in Albania", a Law for "Protection and Conservation of the Albanian Environment", the "Law on Planning".

In order to follow through its intentions, Albania has collaborated with international specialised organisations, governments or experts in this field. To date this collaboration has been with E.B.R.D., with expert groups of the E.C., which have made possible such studies as "Albanian Tourism Guidelines", "Environmental Potential of Tourism Development in Albania" and "Coastal Zone Management Programme" which is financed by the E.C., E.I.B., W.B., U.N.D.P., etc.

The development of tourism will be at both regional and national level. Some tourism development studies, such as in Ksamili and Vrina in southern Albania, facing Corfu, in the Golemi area to the south of Durresi town and in the Velipoja area to the north of the Adriatic sea, etc. Another project on Divjake Karavasta Management has been approved, financed by the PHARE Programme.

Albania is presently experiencing important political and social changes, namely Albanian land ownership of priority tourist development zones. Agricultural land is completely privatised, a part of the unproductive agricultural land, pastures, meadows and woodland on priority tourism development zones, excluding specially protected areas, will be given to the former owners of agricultural and construction land in compensation of their ownership. To achieve long-term conservation, management and land use in balance between public and private of many competitive activities such as agriculture, fishing, tourism, housing and urbanisation phenomena, a system of planning needs to be carried out. New concepts and approaches will be implemented for the management of coastal areas. The first steps are the most important, ones for this reason the Government has organised the study of these zones to repay the ex-owners. These studies will not include the specially protected areas with ecological interest such as the lagoons, the river deltas, sand dunes, reserves, forests and parks of special natural value. The land ownership of the Albanian people of priority tourism development zones and their right to use it will be regulated by the Law and the planning system. Development will be controlled. Investment and building for private or touristic purposes will only be approved by the Territory Adjustment Committee according to the planning studies. Land may be sold to tourist investors or developers. Some specific decisions and rules will be drawn up in order to protect the special protected areas, natural parks and monuments, zones with landscape and archaeological value. The new tourist developments will make possible the development of Albanian coastal areas which for historic and political reasons, up until now, have been the most undeveloped and unpopulated coastal areas in the Mediterranean. For this reason, future orientation of the Albanian people, not including the people who live on the fertile lowland, will move toward the coastline, as this is one of the most essential alternatives for the future economic and urban development of Albania.

ENVIRONMENTAL ISSUES OF ALTERNATIVE TOURISM

Zorica SMILIVA
Assistant to the Minister for the Economy
Former Yugoslav Republic of Macedonia

Ecological problems have recently worsened and have become, moreover, more affected by global economic development. This is due to the methods used in the approach to the problem of pollution. Ecology not only affects the environment but also human society and culture in general.

Different types of tourism are a response to new priorities:

1.   People are now oriented towards a different lifestyle where the importance of quality of the structure of tourism ranks higher than quantity, where intensity replaces extension and the individual has replaced collectivism. Today's tourist seems to appreciate heritage, tradition and ethnic characteristics more.

2.   Health care and the spread of cultural boundaries have promoted a new lifestyle. Interest in new cultures is reflected in nutrition which, from now on, may be used for either curative or preventative purposes. Health and physical exercise have become a part of recreation.

3.   Mass tourism has been abandoned and the tourism industry is reacting accordingly to meet the needs of the individual tourist.

Alternative tourism does not consist of strict planning, it is unpredictable and takes into account the interest in new destinations, as well as adventure, individual tastes, health care and enriching spiritual experiences.

As a result, selective tourism offers holidays with a different approach, in coastal or old towns. Interest in rural tourism is also on the increase, as well as interest in national and leisure parks.

Alternative tourism offers more destinations with fewer visitors in as much as this concept protects nature and offers a closer contact with nature, people and their culture. Tourist activities provided offer direct contact with nature.

The disturbance of the natural balance may have been influenced by the large number of visitors and the inability of those responsible for the targeted areas to deal with them.

The impact of tourism on the environment has three elements:

1.   the vulnerability of different tourist zones with similar tourist activities can seriously threaten the environment,

2.   the capacity of tourist zones calculated according to ecological factors, which at present are overcrowded, manifest ecological disturbances,

3.   the influence of the different kinds of accommodation, traffic and entertainment.

Sustainable development could be considered as a form of development which makes proper use of natural resources and which through its activities, improves the human condition in such a way that improvement can be maintained.

The key factors of sustainable development in tourism are:

1.   the role of organisation and management
2.   the improvement of infrastructures, and
3.   transfers between sectors.

These factors can protect the environment from the threat of an exterior invasion of tourists, interior invasion from new residents and seasonal workers, social tension and the growth of disparities.

The key role of the Government is in the sphere of ecological control and environmental policy. The major elements of this role are:

a.   the control of the technology factor compared with the human factor: the degree to which technology is used in order to obtain greater efficiency as far as cultural heritage is concerned,

b.   the relation between the economy and the human factor: the effect of economic development on the prevention of the destruction of old towns,

c.   the conflict between the (natural) environment and pollution. When an increased tourist trade causes a leap in land prices, the result is the loss of competitiveness between sectors. Yet, a greater investment policy could be destructive to the environment,

d.   the representatives of market management and those who are the opponents of this intervention are in dispute. The Government could adopt a role in adopting efficient legislation in tourism and environmental policy, maintaining political stability, adjusting market policy and connecting this policy to complementary sectors.

Tourism can finance the building of infrastructures, at the same time creating the prerequisites for leisure, cultural and sports facilities that provide certain animation. It also supports agriculture and contributes to rural development. The real issue may be the competition between tourism and other activities, as well as the use of natural resources for tourism goals or for the development of other activities.

In conclusion, the main goal of sustainable development must be to create a coherent dialogue in which different sectors think along the same lines, in order to reach a common approach, and not to contradict each other with opposed ecological policies.

SOME ASPECTS OF THE DEVELOPMENT OF TOURISM ASSOCIATED WITH THE ENVIRONMENT

Tatiana SOBOLEVSKAYA
Ministry of Natural Resources and Environmental Protection
Belarus

The questions which are being discussed at this Colloquy on "Development of Sustainable Tourism and the Environment" are of great interest and use for the Republic of Belarus. Nature study tourism used to be very popular in Belarus. Ten years ago more than eight hundred thousand (800,000) people booked excursions with different tourist organisations every year. More than three hundred thousand (300,000) amateur tourists attended one hundred and eighty (180) tourism clubs. Eleven all-union tourist routes crossed the territory of Belarus. The Republic was popular among the foreign tourists.

Recently however, tourism has declined in Belarus, probably because of the shortage of disposable income of the people in former Soviet republics, the unstable social and political situation in Belarus and the Chernobyl accident. More than 1.7 million hectares of forest (1/7) are situated in zones with different levels of radioactivity (from 1 Cu/km^2 to 40 and more Cu/km^2). Due to the Chernobyl accident, we lost more than three hundred thousand (300,000) hectares of territories which were used for tourism and recreation (20%). Short-term family tourism on days off is now coming to the fore. Tourism in our Republic is becoming more and more commercialised and is directed towards foreign countries. Undoubtedly we believe that the decline of nature tourism in the Republic is temporary because we have a great potential. Tourist and recreational resources include a large number of lakes (more than ten thousand (10,000)), rivers (20.8 thousand), various types of forests filled with berries, nuts and mushrooms, many interesting historical monuments, culture and nature. I should point out that there is a developed network of the protected areas that occupies more than one million hectares (5.2 % of the territory of the Republic) and consists of three "zapovednics", or strict nature reserves, two national parks, which are significant natural areas used for environmental protection research, recreational and educational tourism ("Belovezhskaya Primeval Forest", "Braslavsky Park"), "zakazniks" or system of seventy-five (75) lightly protected natural areas. The latter can protect watersheds, hunting areas, special features and other sites which require a flexible category with some degree of control. The network also includes more than two hundred (200) nature monuments; ancient parks, unique old trees, rare plants, large glacial stones, etc. These protected areas are of great interest and have recreational potential.

A project of interest, "Scheme of the rational allocation of the protected areas", was elaborated in the Republic in 1983 and completed in 1995. According to this Scheme, we planed to set up three national parks, two strict reserves and other kinds of protected areas. We consider that a reasonable combination of recreational, environmental and economical activities are possible under national park conditions.

There are some problems with the conservation of our picturesque lakes and rivers. The large number of small and medium-sized rivers and lakes are susceptible to pollution because there is very little dilution. They are soiled as a result of an agricultural project which shows the strategy for economical and recreational use of the natural resources of the park with the help of marking the social zones, territory planning, changing the direction of the enterprises, arrange special restrictions, learning the tolerance of ecosystems and their capacity.

The first stages of the projects for the three National Parks were elaborated in relation to the development of agriculture, economy, tourism and other activities. But it is difficult to fulfil them under such complicated economic conditions.

The first steps have been taken on the road towards tourism regeneration - sustainable tourism. A special tourism law was elaborated but it has not yet been adopted by the Supreme Soviet of our Republic. The question of the organisation of a special Ministry of Sport and Tourism is being discussed by our Government.

Action is being taken by our reserves and the National Park "Byelovezhskaya Puscha". Specialists from the Council of Europe and some French national parks examined the feasibility conditions for sustainable tourism based on nature watching in the Berezinsky biosphere reserve. Next year the reserve will be welcoming six groups of tourists from France. Hunting tourism has been developed in our famous "Byelovezhskaya Puscha". The Park receives nearly two hundred (200) foreign tourists who are engaged in hunting. Because of the difficulties in crossing boundaries we cannot rapidly develop foreign tourism in this national park.

The Association "EuroAsia" was organised on the basis of one hundred and six (106) tourism organisations and administrations of the former Soviet bloc, in order to restore the indivisible tourism space and further development of the international tourism ties between former republics of the Soviet Union. The representatives of the Belarus tourism organisations are members of this Association. The High School of Tourism in the Belarus State Economic University was created some years ago to prepare specialists in the tourism business.

We understand the problems that exist in the development of tourism and that it is first of all necessary to work out the conception and national programme of sustainable development, especially in the protected areas. It is necessary to develop tourism initially in the territories of the national parks. Mechanisms to ensure that the revenue from tourism is spent within the country should be encouraged. In order to develop foreign tourism, deficiencies in infrastructure, hospitality management and communications will need to be addressed. The partnership between governmental departments, national tourism administration and representative tourism organisations must be established and efforts must be united. We also hope for the assistance from international organisations in solving the problems of tourism.

ENVIRONMENT AND TOURISM -
The Ukrainian experience

Mikhailo D. SYROTA
Parliament, Environmental Commission, Ukraine

In Ukraine we regard tourism as one of the most important sectors of our national economy, as a strong influence in the social, cultural and intellectual development of our people, and as a good starting point for the fruitful evolution of relations and mutual understanding between citizens of various countries and states.

As regards the theme of this Colloquy we should emphasise that now is the time to try to discover more effective ways to integrate environmental protection and sustainable tourism development tasks for their mutual positive influence at both national and international levels.

Beautiful countryside, ancient history with numerous architectural and cultural monuments and a tradition of touristic development all combine to support the theory that Ukraine would readily integrate with other European countries.

Ukraine itself covers an area of 604,000 squ. km with a population of more than 52 million. It encompasses forest land, the steppe-forest, the steppe and broad-leaved forest zones. We have the Carpathian and Crimean mountain systems. Ukrainian flora consists of some 5,000 species, its fauna of more than 45,000 species.

As for the network of reserve territories, they include 6365 of the most valuable scientific and environmental positions with a total area of 1,465,615 hectares, which amounts to 2.26% of Ukraine's territory.

The Ukrainian Parliament has recognised that the extensive industrial agricultural development (arable lands account for 70% in many regions) and densely populated areas considerably influence the level of anthropogenic impact in Ukraine, resulting in a veritable ecological disaster. According to the latest assessment, only 32% of natural flora has survived. The ecological situation in Ukraine has especially worsened as a result of the Chernobyl disaster - Cs-137 contaminated zone with the radiation level surpassing 1 ku per square Km over an area of 40,000 Km (over 8% of the total territory).

All these factors are negative for tourism development. Last year however, more than 800 000 foreigners visited Ukraine. Less than 1,5 million people work in the tourist industry.

The fundamentals of environmental protection are stipulated in Ukraine at Constitutional level as environmental laws were rapidly developed in the past few years. This legislation includes a basic Environmental Protection Law, Land, Water, Forest Codes, Air and Fauna Protection Laws, the Law on the Natural Reserve Fund approved by Verkhovna Rada, the Ukrainian Parliament. Special regulations were adopted by the Cabinet of Ministers - Government.

On the basis of our national and international experience we will try to finish the general formation of our environmental legislative system as soon as possible. At present, our Parliament and Government are co-operating with both Ukrainian and foreign scientists on draft laws on plant protection and waste management and a long-term State environmental programme.

Some months ago, Ukraine adopted a law on tourism. Our Commission on the Environment took an active role in its preparation. We tried to implement as much as possible the achievements of the countries with a good track record in this field. This law determines the main principles and tasks of tourism in Ukraine, the function of the State and the rights and obligations of tourist organizations independent of their interests.

We think that on this legal basis, it will be possible to achieve some positive results in the sphere of environmental protection and tourism. We hope to actively participate in international co-operation, a more effective role in tourism to lead towards economic development of our country and on this basis, the improvement of the environmental situation. A pleasant environment is a very effective way to increase benefits from tourism. We need to place more emphasis on the stimulation of special environmental tourism.

APPENDIX 1

CO-OPERATION PROGRAMME
WITH CENTRAL AND EASTERN EUROPEAN COUNTRIES

COLLOQUY ON "SUSTAINABLE TOURISM DEVELOPMENT"

9 November 1995

<u>Morning</u> Chaired by: Mr Nicos S. GEORGIADES

09h00   Opening of Colloquy
          Address by the Minister of the Environment, Mr Avraam LOUCA

09h30   Presentation of the Council of Europe's Co-operation Programme with countries of Central and Eastern Europe and outline of specific activities relating to the development of sustainable tourism, Mrs Hélène Bouguessa, Council of Europe

10h00   Sustainable tourism: an economic choice and the conservation/development of natural and cultural resources
          Exposé on the general theme by the General Rapporteur of the Colloquy
          (Suzanne THIBAL, Secrétaire Général d'EUROTER)

10h30   Tourism development policy and environmental protection in Cyprus Tourism development in Cyprus, Patroclos A. APOSTOLIDES, Minister for Agriculture, Natural Resources and the Environment, Cyprus Tourism Organisation

11h00   Break

11h30   Mr. Hermes KLOKKARIS, Town Planning Department, Nicosia

12h00   Discussion

12h30   Lunch

<u>Après-midi</u>   Chaired by: Mr Patroclos A. APOSTOLIDES

14h00   The Protection of nature - Tourism - Local Population: a delicate balance, Case study of North-East Hungary (M. Janos LERNER, Aggtelek National Park, Hungary)

14h45   Mr Robert LANQUAR, Blue Plan for the Mediterranean Zone

15h30   Pause

16h00   The protection of the countryside and the development of tourism in Estonia, Toomas KOKOVKIN

16h45   Discussion on the themes of the day

19h00   Reception given by the Ministry of Agriculture, Natural Resources and the Environment

---

10 November 1995

Morning Chaired by: Mr Patrolos A. APOSTOLIDES

09h30   Environmental policy and Management in Cyprus, Exposé by Mr N.S. GEORGIADES, Director, Environment Service, Ministry of Agriculture, Natural Resources and Environment

10h15   Ms Xenia LOIZIDOU, Coastal erosion and protective measures, Cypriot Public Works Department, Nicosia,

11h00   Break

11h30   Mr SHACKLEFORD, Presentation on the development of tourism in Central and Eastern European countries and the identification of its repercussions on the environment, Organisation Mondiale du Tourisme/World Tourism Organisation

12h15   Pollution: Legal means for the control of waste and sewage, Anthony ELLUL, Malta

13h00   Lunch

Afternoon   Chaired by: Mr Nicos S. GEORGIADES

14h30   M. Carlos PINTO, Member of Parliament, Member of the Commission for the Environment, Land Management and of Local Authorities of the Parliamentary Assembly of the Council of Europe

15h15   The Coast : old human settlement but growing human pressure, Louis BRIGAND, Lecturer in Geography, University of Eastern Brittany (France)

16h30   Control of tourist development liable to have significant consequences on the environment: national, regional and local planning policy
            Anthony ELLUL, Malte

17h15   Presentations by the Central and Eastern European Representatives

           The case of Albania, Genc METOHU, Architect, Director of the Department for regional tourism projects, Ministry of Tourism and Construction

           Environmental Issues of Alternative Tourism, Republic of Macedonia, Zorica SMILEVA, Deputy Economic Minister

           Some aspects of the development of tourism associated with the environment, Tatiana SOBOLEVSKAYA, Ministry for Natural Resources and the Protection of the Environment, Republic of Belarus

           Environment and Tourism - The Ukrainian experience, Mikhailo D. SYROTA, Commission of the Environment, Parliament

17h45   Overview of the presentations and discussions during the Colloquy (Suzanne THIBAL)

18h00   Closure of the Colloquy

---

11 November 1995

           Excursion to Limassol and Paphos organised and paid for by the Cyprus Tourist Organisation.

APPENDIX 2

LISTE DES PARTICIPANTS / LIST OF PARTICIPANTS

RAPPORTEURS (in alphabetic order / par ordre alphabétique)

M. Patroclos A. APOSTOLIDES, Tourism Organisation, 19 Limassol Avenue, PO Box 4535, Nicosia, Tel. (357) 2/33 77 15   Fax (357) 2/33 16 44

M. Louis BRIGAND, Université de Bretagne Occidentale, Faculté des Sciences, Laboratoire Géosystèmes, 6, avenue Le Gorgeu, BP 809, F 29285 Brest Cedex
Tel. (33) 98 01 66 88   Fax (33) 98 01 66 26

M. Anthony ELLUL, Planning Authority, Floriana, PO Box 200, Valletta CMR 01, Malta
Tel. (356) 24 09 76   Fax (356) 22 48 46

Mr. Nicos S. GEORGIADES, Director, Environment Service, Ministry of Agriculture, Natural Resources and Environment, Nicosia
Tel. (357) 2/302 883   Fax (357) 2/445 156

Mr. Avraam LOUCA, Permanent Secretary, Ministry of Agriculture, Natural Resources and Environment, Nicosia
Tel. (357) 2/302 883   Fax (357) 2/445 156

Mr. Hermes KLOKKARIS, Town and Country Planning Department, Nicosia
Fax: (357) 2 367570

Mr. Toomas KOKOVKIN, Research Director, Hiiumaa Centre of the West-Estonian Archipelago Biosphere Reserve, Kärdla, EE 3200, Estonia
Tel. (372) 46 96 260, 96 276   Fax (372) 46 96 269

M. Robert LANQUAR, 26 Dufrénoy, 75116 PARIS, France
Tel. (33) 1 45 04 56 96   Fax. (33) 1 45 04 57 05

Dr. Janos LERNER, Inspector of Tourism, Aggtelek National Park,
H - 3758 Josvafo Tengerszem oldal 1
Tel/Fax (36) 48 350 006

Ms. Xenia LOIZIDOU, Cypriot Public Works Department, Nicosia,

Mr SHACKLEFORD, Organisation Mondiale du Tourisme/World Tourism Organisation, C. Capitan Haya 42, MADRID, E - 28020
Tel. (34) 571 06 28   Fax (34) 1 571 37 33

GENERAL RAPPORTEUR

Mlle Suzanne THIBAL, Secrétaire Général d'EUROTER, 82, rue François-Rolland, F-94130 Nogent-sur-Marne
Tel. (33) 1/45 14 64 21   Fax (33) 1/43 94 91 44

PARTICIPANTS

ALBANIA / ALBANIE

Mr. Genc METOHU, Chief of the Section for Touristic Regional Projects, Ministry of Tourism, Bulevardi "Deshmoret e Kombit", Tirana, Albania
Tel. (355) 42 252 26   Fax (355) 42 279 31.

BELARUS

Mrs Tatiana SOBOLEVSKAYA, Ministry for the Environment, Kollektornaia Street 10, 220050 MINSK
Tel. (375) 172 206 691   Fax (375) 172 20 55 83

BULGARIA / BULGARIE

CZECH REPUBLIC / REPUBLIQUE TCHEQUE

Dr Jan STURSA, Admnistration of Krkonose National Park, 54311 Vrchlabi-Zamek, Czech Republic   Tel. (42) 438 21011   Fax (42) 438 23095

CROATIA / CROATIE

Mr. Radenko DEZELIC, Counsellor in the State Administration for Protection of Cultural and Natural Heritage of the Republic of Croatia, Ilica 44/II, 10000 Zagreb, Croatia
Tel. (385) 1 4342 022, 432 023   Fax (385) 1 431 515

ESTONIA / ESTONIE   (Apologised for absence/excusé)

Mr. Kalju KUKK, Director of General Department, Ministry of the Environment, Toompuiestee 24, EE 0100 Tallinn, Estonia
Tel. (372) 6 45 58 58   Fax (372) 6453310

HONGRIE / HUNGARY

Dr. Janos TARDY, Deputy Secretary of State, Nature Conservation Authority of the Ministry for Environment and Regional Policy, H 1121 Budapest, Költö u. 21
Tel. (36) 1 175 1093   Fax (36) 1 175 7557

LATVIA / LETTONIE

Mrs. Aria ANDRIKSONE, Head of the Tourism Division, Ministry of Environmental Protection and Regional Development,Peldu Street 25, Riga, LV 1494
Tel. (371) 8 820 442   Fax (371) 8 820 442

LITUANIE / LITHUANIA

Mrs. Giedré GODIENE, Senior Geographist of the Landscape Division, Environmental Protection Ministry, Juozapaviciaus str.9, 2600 Vilnius, Lithuania
Tel. (370) 2 72 31 53   Fax (370) 2 72 80 20

"FORMER YUGOSLAV REPUBLIC OF MACEDONIA /EX-REPUBLIQUE YOUGOSLAVE DE MACEDOINE"

Ms. Zorica SMILEVA, Assistant to the Minister of Economy in charge of Tourism, Bote Bocevskuy St. No. 9, 91000 SKOPJE
Tel. (99) 389 91 220 655   Fax (99) 389 91 232 235

MOLDOVA

Mr. Mihai CAMERZAN, Directeur-adjoint de la Compagnie d'Etat "Moldova-Tur", Asociatia Nationala pentru Turism "Moldova-Tur", Hotel "National", bd Stefan cel Mare 4, 277058 Chisinau, Republica Moldova,
Tel. (373) 2 22 23 27   Fax (373) 2 26 25 86

POLAND / POLOGNE

Mr. Zbigniew NIEWIADOMSKI, Bieszczadzki National Park, Wolosate 12/2, 38 714 Ustrzyki Gorne, c/o Ministry of Protection of Environment, Natural Resources and Forests, National Service of National Parks, ul. Wawelska 52/54, 00 922 Warszawa, Poland
Tel/Fax (48) 22 25 57 48 or 25 14 93

ROMANIA / ROUMANIE   (Apologised for absence/excusée)

Mrs. Speranta IANCULESCU, Directrice, Direction des Stratégies et Législation de l'Environnement, Ministry of Environment, Liertatii Bld. n° 121, Bucharest
Tel. (40) 1 410 63 94   Fax (40) 1 410 63 94

Dipl. eng. Nicolae CIOBANU, Third Secretary, Economic and Commercial Affairs Embassy of Romania, 83 Kennedy Avenue, Nicosia
Tel. 02 379303   Fax. 02 379121

FEDERATION OF RUSSIA / FEDERATION DE RUSSIE

SLOVAK REPUBLIC / REPUBLIQUE SLOVAQUE

Miss Katarina KRALIKOVA, Slovak Agency for the Environment, Tajovského 28, 975 90 Banska Bystrica, Slovakia
Tel. (42) 88 360 34   Fax (42) 88 335 531

SLOVENIA / SLOVENIE

UKRAINE

Mr. M.D. SYROTA, Deputy Head of Ukrainian Parliament Ecological Commission, c/o Ministry for Environmental Protection and Nuclear Safety of Ukraine, 5 Khreshchatyk str., 252001 Kiev-1, Ukraine Tel. (380) 44 228 00 44   Fax (380) 44 228 29 22

PARLIAMENTARY ASSEMBLY OF THE COUNCIL OF EUROPE/ ASSEMBLÉE PARLEMENTAIRE DU CONSEIL DE L'EUROPE

M. Carlos PINTO, Député, Membre de la Commission de l'Environnement, de l'Aménagement du Territoire et des Pouvoirs Locaux de l'Assemblée Parlementaire / MP, Member of the Committee on Environment, Regional Planning and Local Authorities of the Parliamentary Assembly, P.O.Box 185, P - 6202 Covilha
Tel. (351) 75/34 551   Fax (351) 1/395 59 40

M. René COUVEINHES   (Apologised for absence/excusé)
Député, Membre de l'Assemblée Parlementaire du Conseil de l'Europe, Assemblée Nationale, 75355 PARIS 07 SP

SECRETARIAT DU CONSEIL DE L'EUROPE / COUNCIL OF EUROPE SECRETARIAT

Mme Hélène BOUGUESSA, Division de la Conservation et de la Gestion de l'Environnement/Environmental Conservation and Management Division, Council of Europe, F 67075 Strasbourg, Tél. (33) 88 41 22 64, Fax (33) 88 41 27 84

Miss Julie SMITH, Division de la Conservation et de la Gestion de l'Environnement/Environmental Conservation and Management Division, Council of Europe, F 67075 Strasbourg, Tél. (33) 88 41 32 02, Fax (33) 88 41 27 84